Bridging THE Gap

How to Create More Emotional Intimacy in Your Marriage

Bridging the Gap

*How to Create More Emotional
Intimacy in Your Marriage*

Christina Shelley Albrecht

sΔp
Summit View Publishing
Orem, Utah

Cover image *Beautiful Botanical Garden* by Katrina Brown © Dreamstime.com.
Cover design and page layout by Jennie Williams

© 2017 Christina Shelley Albrecht

All rights reserved. No part of this book may be reproduced in any manner or form without written permission from the author.

Summit View Publishing
Orem, Utah 84097
www.SummitViewPublishing.com or www.sviewp.com

ISBN-13: 978-0-9818692-1-6
ISBN-10: 0-9818692-1-1

Printed in the United States of America

10 9 8 7 6 5 4 3 2 1

This book is printed on acid free paper.

To all my friends—known and unknown—
who long for closer, happier relationships
with their spouses.
May this book assist you
in creating your own version
of happily ever after.

Contents

This Book Is for You If 1

Part 1
The Challenging Marriage Relationship

My Story: Why I Still Believe in *Happily Ever After* 5

What *Happily Ever After* Looks Like in the Real World 11

What Do the Words *Husband* and *Wife* Mean to You? 13

Who's Nurturing Your Marriage? 15

How Relationships Are Built, Why They Deteriorate,
and What to Do Next 19

Part 2
The Amazing Love Log
How to Take Your Marriage to the Next Level

How the Love Log Came to Be 37

Setting Yourself Up for Success 41

Red Cars and Orange Butterflies 47

Keeping Your Experiments Confidential 51

What to Record in Your Love Log 53

Designing Your Daily Connection Plan 59

What about Making Monthly and Yearly Plans? 63

Customizing Your Love Log 67

How to Quickly Reconnect When One of You Loses It 69

How Long Will It Take to See Results? 71

Conclusion: *Celebrate Your Marriage!* 73

Appendix A: Using a Rating Scale to Determine How to Proceed 75

Appendix B: How to Get the Best Mileage Out of Your Weekly Planning and Talk Time 81

Recommended Resources and Helpful Quotations 85

Notes 99

Index 101

Acknowledgments 103

This Book Is for You If...

This book is for you . . .

- If you have ever thought, "I'm a good person and my spouse is a good person, so why is this marriage thing so hard?"
- If you feel distant and disconnected from your spouse but believe you could reconnect if you just knew how to do it.
- If you feel like you have a pretty good marriage but would like it to be even better.
- If you are willing to invest 5–10 minutes a day making notes and planning different ways to rebuild or strengthen your relationship.

This book is NOT for you . . .

- If you are in a physically abusive relationship.
- If you are dealing with addictions, infidelity, or mental disorders.
- If you are truly on the brink of divorce.

If you are experiencing any of these things in your relationship, I encourage you to seek help from a competent counselor. Ask others in your community for recommendations. You will be surprised how quickly you will find assistance when you start looking for it.

I also highly recommend that you read *The Divorce Remedy: The Proven 7-Step Program for Saving Your Marriage* by Michele Weiner-Davis.

> *Investing a little time in your emotional connection will not only strengthen your marriage, it will also energize you to more effectively tackle other challenges and responsibilities in your life.*

If you're concerned that working on your marriage will take too much time and effort, consider this: Improving your marriage is very energizing! Investing a little time in your emotional connection will not only strengthen your marriage, it will also energize you to more effectively tackle other challenges and responsibilities in your life. It's a wonderful bonus!

PART 1

The Challenging Marriage Relationship

Love may be blind,
but marriage is a real eye opener!
—*Anonymous*

We don't have to be perfect
to be perfect for each other.
—*Anonymous*

Marriage is the hardest work you'll ever do,
but it is also the best work you'll ever do.
—*Audrey Knighton* (my grandmother)

My Story: Why I Still Believe in Happily Ever After

I grew up in a religious community that focused a lot on marriage and family. I was one of six children, and most of our neighbors were also two-parent families with several children. As a child I looked forward to getting married and having a family of my own, but during my teenage years I gradually became aware of the marital pain and divorce going on in the world. Not only did I notice it in some families in my neighborhood, I also often heard that 50% of the marriages in the United States end in divorce. SCARY!!!

When I started dating, I was careful to go out with guys of good character who shared my beliefs and values. As I got older I prayerfully looked for a man who would be a good match for me—someone I especially enjoyed being with and who also cared about the things I felt were important in life. I wanted to be absolutely sure I had God's blessing on my marriage.

My husband and I met at church, and I was immediately drawn to his character and his intelligence. We seemed to have a lot in common because, like me, he was devoted to our religion, he loved to read, he attended the same university that I did, he loved language and culture, and he had a strong work ethic. He was a landscaper and arborist, who loved to do physical work, spend time in the outdoors, work on his old classic car, and do home improvement projects. So as part of our dating, we often worked on trees, cars, or house projects together.

For about a year, we dated, talked, worked and played together, gradually developing a deep appreciation and love for each other. We were both hesitant to talk about marriage, but after lots of time and prayer, we decided to go for it.

Marrying my husband meant moving from a university town with an academic, intellectual, and high-tech focus, to a rural area of southwestern Colorado where the main focus is agriculture. I was nervous about the move, but I was also excited. I'd always wanted to be a "country girl" like my mom and my grandmother. They had both grown up working in the garden, canning produce, and caring for animals. Finally, I would have a chance to live my country girl dream.

Unfortunately, I soon discovered that my new reality did not match my dream at all. Instead of happily singing while I cooked, cleaned, canned, and worked in the garden, I constantly felt frustrated. I didn't have as many useful skills as I had thought, and developing them was much harder than I expected. I found that I not only lacked a green thumb, I actually had a black thumb!

To make matters worse, a severe drought hit our area my first year in Colorado. No clouds. No rain. No water in the well. And the raging winds often created dust walls that stretched from the ground to the sky. I quickly realized that being a "country girl" did *not* fill my heart with joy like I'd thought it would.

However, my most difficult realization was that my husband and I had much less in common than I had ever imagined.

He prefers a quiet, private life. I thrive on being with lots of different people. We both work hard, but he is laser-focused, fast, and efficient. I, on the other hand, take a slow and steady approach to most things. I can spend all day writing, studying and working on the computer, but I don't have half the energy and stamina for physical labor that my husband does.

From the very beginning, I struggled with the unpredictability of my husband's work schedule. My dad worked at a university, so our family always knew when he would leave for work and when he would be home. But my husband, like his father, is self-employed. The random schedule was totally normal to him, but for me, it was a constant frustration. To say this was difficult would be a serious understatement. It took me more than a decade to quit longing for a more regular routine.

And then there was the question of how to go from living near my own family to integrating into my husband's family. We lived within a few miles of his parents, his siblings and their families, his aunts, uncles, cousins, and *all* of their children. It seemed like almost everyone I met was somehow related to us! Although they were generally welcoming, I missed the comfort of being around my own family and often felt like a fish out of water.

While my husband had been happy to leave the bustle of the city and return to the familiar setting of his hometown, his previous work, and his family, I now felt lonely, incompetent, and insecure. I had thought I was adaptable and easy going, but I had no idea how to cope with so many changes. I'm sure my husband wondered what had happened to the cheerful, capable girl he thought he'd married.

So there we were, two good people, both surprised to find that we actually had very little in common, and both disappointed because things weren't working out the way we had expected. We shared the goal of building a wonderful home and family together, but each of us felt frustrated and unsatisfied.

In spite of our many differences, we did the best we could. We shared some good times, but we simply didn't have the skills we needed to create a strong, nurturing marriage. We were often overwhelmed by the day-to-day demands of his self-employment, not to mention all the work needing to be done on our own property.

Then our first baby was born. She brought with her a wonderful new dimension of love and joy, but caring for her brought a previously-unknown amount of fatigue. My husband worked hard every day and I worked hard caring for our daughter and our home every day. Unfortunately, our positive time together as a couple decreased. We were usually so tired or stressed when we had an opportunity to be together that it was hard to reconnect. As time went on, we became more and more distant. We got to the point where we both felt overworked, underappreciated, and generally unloved.

After several years and another baby, we finally sat down and had a serious talk. Even though we weren't happy with how things were going in our marriage, we were committed to each other and to our little daughters. We agreed that we needed to stop criticizing each other, and we also decided to have a weekly meeting for planning, catching up, and addressing any issues that needed our attention.

Both of these things helped tremendously, and within a few months we began to feel like friends again.

Over the next few years our relationship was more peaceful, but we still weren't as close or as happy as I believed we could be. At one point, I decided to work with a coach who taught communication and relationship skills. She helped me discover some pivotal techniques that improved our relationship significantly. I also attended a series of relationship classes taught by a seasoned counselor whose insights gave me a whole new perspective on my marriage.

As I incorporated what I had learned, my relationship with my husband improved, but I still wanted a closer connection. I decided to try again and search for a way to bridge our emotional gap. I read several marriage books, took lots of notes, and began to experiment to see if I could figure out what would help us feel more connected on a daily basis. Each night I made a few notes about the experiments I had tried that day and how well they had worked.

I was amazed at the results! Within a week my husband and I were thoroughly enjoying each other and spending more time together. I continued to try out different ideas, and after just a few months, I felt like we were living our own unique version of *happily ever after*.

While I mostly kept what I was doing to myself, I would occasionally share a fun experience with my mom or with one of my close friends. Then one day my mom called me, asking if I might have suggestions for her friend, Linda (name changed), who was feeling discouraged because her marriage was at an all-time low.

I immediately put together an email for Linda with notes from the marriage books I'd read. I also explained how I had experimented to see what would create the best connection between my husband and me. Then I encouraged her to be prayerful and to try some experimenting of her own.

After reading through my notes, Linda immediately dove into the impromptu program I had outlined for her. The following week I got another phone call from my mom. She told me that Linda's heart had been totally transformed, and that her connection with her husband felt amazingly better.

Linda has emailed me several times to thank me for my help. She told my mom that her inner dialog has completely changed and that she feels happier in her marriage now than she had for many years. Occasionally, she still calls to tell my mom about a new experiment she is trying or a positive change that is happening in her relationship.

Since sending my notes to Linda I've had the opportunity to share the ideas and tools in this book with others. Those who have applied them in their relationships have been very happy with the results. Thanks to the persistent encouragement and support I've received, I now have the opportunity to share these things with you. May they help you create your very own version of *happily ever after*.

What Happily Ever After Looks Like in the Real World

Most love stories are romanticized to a fault. In old fairytales, present-day movies, and everything in between we see two people meet, fall in love, get married, and live *happily ever after*. We get the impression that these two people will forever enjoy the euphoria of being in love.

But when we look at our modern-day society, we see a markedly different picture. Yes, we do see some happily married couples, but we also see many unhappy couples, couples who have divorced, couples who have divorced and tried again with someone new, and even couples who have divorced and remarried each other. Obviously, in real life, *happily ever after* doesn't magically happen just because two people make it to the altar.

What does *happily ever after* look like anyway? The stories never say! But thankfully, some experienced researchers and marriage counselors do.

John Gottman, a well-known marriage therapist and author, says happily-married couples spend most of their time in a state he calls "positive sentiment override."[1] This means that you have so many good (or positive) things going in your marriage that they far outweigh the inevitable negative things.

It's like Stephen Covey's concept of having an Emotional Bank Account[2] with a very large positive balance. You have many, many positive memories, thoughts, and experiences in your account, and you're always depositing more by thinking, saying, and doing positive things that strengthen your marriage. When there's a withdrawal, or in other words a negative interaction in your marriage, your Emotional Bank Account can easily absorb the hit. You might not even really notice when little negative things happen because the positive things wash them away before they have a chance to stick.

Regardless of what the movies or fairytales say, don't be fooled! "Happily ever after" does not mean "happy together all the time with no irritations whatsoever." That expectation leads to frustration and disappointment. Instead, embrace reality and let it fuel your optimism. The truth is that two normal, imperfect people can have their share of ups and downs and still learn to be pretty darn happy together. The purpose of this book is to help you as you work toward creating your own version of *happily ever after*.

> *"Happily ever after" does not mean "happy together all the time with no irritations whatsoever."*

What Do the Words Husband and Wife Mean to You?

In this book, we are going to zoom in on one thing: the personal relationship between you and your spouse.

While our roles frequently overlap, don't confuse being a husband or wife with being a provider, a maid, or a parent.

A *wife* is not a slave to her family, a maid-of-all-work, a co-provider, or a business partner. A *wife* is not a mother. Wives may do some or all of those things, but at the very core, that is not who and what a wife is.

> **A *wife* is an individual,
> a friend, a lover, and a life partner.**

A *husband* is not a slave to his family who always has to go to work to provide. He's not a sperm donor. He's not a babysitter, co-worker, or business partner. A *husband* is not a father. Yes, husbands do lots of things for their families and wear many hats just as wives do, but at the very core, that isn't who and what a husband is.

> **A *husband* is an individual,
> a friend, a lover, and a life partner.**

Most couples marry because they love to be together. They are very special friends. They love feeling heard, accepted, and understood. They feel valued and admired. They love working and playing together. But after they get married, many things change. They have different responsibilities and focuses. They usually spend less time together and they tend to disagree more than they did before they were married. Misunderstandings and hurts occur, and all these things impact the emotional connection they feel. Even though they don't like what's happening to their relationship, most couples don't know what to do about it.

Who's Nurturing Your Marriage?

While I was researching healthy marriages, a recurring theme came up that really bothered me. These quotations from John Gottman are just a couple of examples. He said,

> More than 80 percent of the time, it's the wife who brings up sticky marital issues, while the husband tries to avoid discussing them. This isn't a symptom of a troubled marriage—it's true in most happy marriages as well.[3]

> Usually one member of a couple tends to take the lead in sniffing out trouble. More often than not it is the wife.[4]

As I contemplated these ideas, I started to feel a familiar resentment bubble up as I remembered times I had asked myself questions like:

Why do I have to be the one to babysit this marriage?

Why can't he take some initiative and figure out how to help us get closer?

Why do I have to do all the work in this relationship?

But then another thought came to me. Instead of resenting what apparently is my natural role, what if I embraced it? What if I willingly took the reins in my relationship and looked for totally new ways to create greater happiness in my life instead of worrying about what my husband was or wasn't doing? Wouldn't I be more likely to get the results I'm looking for?

This was a major mental shift for me because I previously thought I had tried everything and nothing had worked. I worried that no matter what I tried, nothing would *ever* work. However, in the course of reading books about successful marriages, I realized that there were several things I could do that were very different from what I'd tried before. Though I *had* tried a lot of different things in the past, in hindsight, I discovered that they were all versions of the same technique: verbal communication.

So, what if I stopped talking so much and started *doing* different things and *observing* how I felt?

Interesting concept!

But I still couldn't help asking myself "Shouldn't my husband have to help somehow?"

Then I read the following paragraph in *The Divorce Remedy* by Michele Weiner-Davis.

> If you are someone who has requested, nagged, or begged your partner to become more involved in marriage-improving activities, quit it now. *Although your spouse doesn't know it yet*, s/he is about to join forces with you to make things better. *When you tip over the first domino in your marriage, relationship change will be right around the corner.*[5]

That was the encouragement I needed to let go of my resentment. As I began nurturing my marriage on a daily basis, my husband started to initiate connecting conversations and activities, too. He invited me to spend time doing fun things with him and we also spent more time talking about our family and about our hopes and dreams.

I no longer felt that I was the only one working on our marriage. I was amazed that he naturally engaged in our relationship solely in response to my positive efforts. When I "tipped over the first domino," relationship change really was right around the corner. My hope is that the suggestions in *Bridging the Gap* will help you tip over the first domino in your relationship and that you will also experience rewarding positive changes.

How Relationships Are Built, Why They Deteriorate, and What to Do Next

Like most people, I have "hot buttons" that trigger an intensely negative reaction when they get pushed. Well, one evening, before I learned about the principles I discuss in this book, my husband unintentionally pushed two of my hot buttons one right after the other and I completely lost it. I angrily said a few things I wish I hadn't, and then I quickly left the room. When I tried to apologize the next day, it did not go well, and between the two experiences, I took a mental and emotional nose-dive.

For months I had been working with a coach who teaches communication skills developed by Marshall Rosenberg. His work is called Compassionate Communication or Nonviolent Communication (NVC).[6] I had invested a tremendous amount of time, effort, and money into learning and practicing the relationship skills she was teaching me. My marriage and family life had improved significantly and I was feeling very happy with how things were going. But then, the one time I wasn't perfectly in control, everything fell apart. It felt like all my work had been for nothing. I began to wonder if I could ever really make a difference, regardless of how hard I tried.

Fortunately, a couple of weeks later I was able to attend an adult education class taught by a wonderful presenter named

Carrie Wrigley. Carrie had been a counselor for over 20 years and had helped many people rejuvenate their marriages.

In her class titled "Creating Love: Building and Maintaining a Heartfelt Connection with Your Spouse and Loved Ones," Carrie taught that solid relationships are built on four basic building blocks: time, talk, trust, and touch. She called these the 4 T's. She explained that when relationships erode, the best chance for successfully rebuilding them is to focus on implementing time, talk, trust, and touch, one at a time *in that specific order*. (See diagrams of the 4 T's.)

When I heard this concept, it relieved a lot of stress for me. I could look back over my marriage and see how right she was—both about how our relationship was originally built and about why my husband and I had become so distant. I felt hopeful. It helped me so much to hear that if I just focused on one thing at a time and let the upcoming steps wait their turn, our relationship could be rebuilt. This new plan gave me the clarity and strength I needed to try again.

THE 4 T'S
How Relationships Are Built and Rebuilt

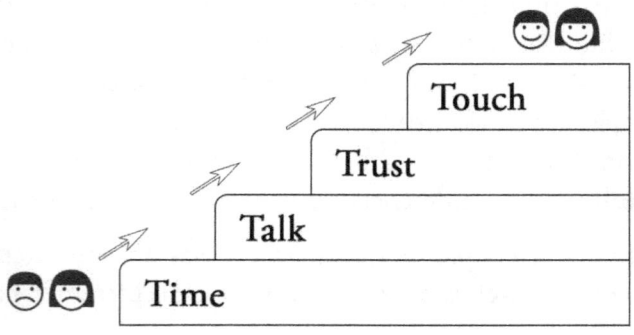

As I began applying what Carrie had taught, I was surprised at how quickly our relationship improved. I didn't try to reconnect by forcing conversation or affection like I had in the past. I just focused on keeping a positive mindset and spending time together. Less than a week later, I felt myself wanting to open up more, and soon we were talking comfortably. The trust and touch naturally followed.

Because the 4 T's made such a remarkable difference in my marriage, I really wanted to share them with others. I contacted Carrie requesting permission to write about them on my blog, and she encouraged me to share them in any way I could, so here they are.

Time

Think about how *any* solid relationship starts. It always starts with a large investment of time. Friendships, marriage partners, parent-child relationships, business partners, you name it. Time is always invested when getting to know each other.

THE 4 T'S
How Relationships Erode

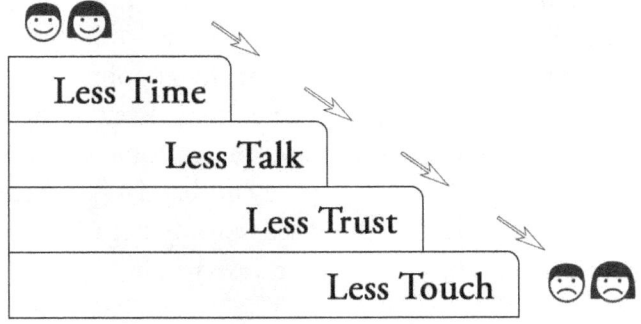

When relationships erode, the first thing to go is almost always time together. In the case of marriage, this decrease of time often happens for the best of reasons. Maybe it's a great career opportunity, or a new baby, or a new position in your church or community. Of course, other not-so-great reasons can decrease the time couples have together, like when one or both partners spend a lot of time chatting on the phone with friends, surfing the Internet, participating in social media, playing computer or video games, watching TV, and so on.

When you want to rebuild or enhance a relationship, intentional time investment must come first. If a relationship is pretty rocky, avoid the temptation to try to "talk things out" right away or to try to convince your spouse that you can be trusted because you frequently say, "I love you." I found it works much better to focus only on spending positive time together. No words necessary!

To spend *positive* time together you need to watch your thoughts. The way you habitually think about your marriage and your spouse makes a huge difference in the quality of your relationship.

During a particularly intense conflict with my husband, I was feeling extremely frustrated and upset. I already had a session scheduled with my NVC coach, so I decided to get her take on our situation. When I went in for my appointment a few days later, she listened as I explained why I felt so agitated. Then she asked a few questions and shared some insights that helped me see the situation—and my husband—in an entirely different light. Suddenly I could see that my negative mindset had caused both of us a lot of unnecessary pain.

This experience brought home to me the importance of maintaining a positive mindset. I immediately started paying closer attention to my thoughts. I noticed what I thought about my husband and about my marriage in general. When I caught my thoughts going down a negative path, I'd stop myself. Then I'd take a few deep breaths, consciously adjust my perspective, and refocus my attention on positive things about my marriage.

I learned that if I wanted a magnificent marriage, I had to train myself to *think* positively as well as to speak and act positively. I will share more about how to develop this wonderful skill in a later chapter, but for now, just be aware of your thoughts and try to feed the good while starving the bad.

One girl I worked with had a particularly strained relationship. When she learned about the 4 T's, she told me she was relieved that she wouldn't have to talk to her husband for a while. To begin, she set a goal just to spend some positive time in the same room with him a few times each day. She also set a goal to watch her thoughts and keep them as positive as she could. She told me that sometimes her relationship felt so tense she could only commit to being in the same room with him for five minutes at a time. She would take a breath, say a prayer, walk into the room, glance at the clock, and then just try to stay in a good frame of mind for the whole five minutes.

She said that during those few minutes, she deliberately focused her thoughts on things that made her smile, and she also engaged pleasantly with her children. If her husband spoke to her, she responded, but she didn't try to initiate a conversation. When her five minutes were up, she would nonchalantly walk out of the room and immediately do something that was nurturing to her.

It wasn't very long before she felt a little less vulnerable, so she started spending more time with her husband. Over the next few days, they took a short walk, went to the store, watched a movie, and read aloud together. She noticed that her husband seemed less stressed and more interested in her. She began enjoying the time they were spending together, and a week later, she found herself wanting to open up verbally. So she moved to the next step.

Talk

Good communication is an essential part of a healthy relationship. For most women (not all, but most), talking is their preferred way to connect, and they do a lot of it! Face to face, on the phone, in the car—wherever they are, they're usually talking. My husband used to joke, "A happy Tina is a talking Tina." Yep! And when I'm not talking, I'm singing, reading, or writing. I love to communicate! And most of my female friends are right there with me.

HOWEVER...

A man usually gets all talked out long before his wife's desire to connect through words is satisfied. His eyes may start to glaze over when his wife is barely getting warmed up for a good, long conversation.

What to do?

You can always stop talking so much and see what happens.

When I tried that, I was fascinated by the results: my husband started asking me what I was thinking! He'd never had to wonder before because my thoughts were always being verbalized. I also observed that when I talked less, he often seemed more relaxed.

For many husbands, lots of words can feel overwhelming and stressful, especially when they are trying to get out the door in the morning, or when they are just coming home from a job that's draining. Wives often want to connect at these moments by reviewing schedules, sharing news, or asking for clarification about something. Isn't it ironic that sometimes the very thing we instinctively do to try to connect has the exact opposite effect?

This may sound like I'm saying, "If you want to be happily married, don't talk to your spouse, or at least don't talk very much." That's not at all the case. After all, *talking* is one of the 4 T's of relationship building. Actually, the healthier and happier you are in your marriage, the more frequently and naturally you and your spouse will talk. However, a wife needs to know her husband well enough to know when talking has the best chance of being connecting for both of them. She needs to have a good idea of how much talking her husband can handle, and she needs to learn not to take it personally when he doesn't want to talk as much as she does.

Special Tips from the Experts

Intentionally Cultivate the Positive. In her class, Carrie Wrigley mentioned that wives should try to do about 85% of their talking with people other than their husbands. Yes, a husband is a friend, but women need to have other friends to talk to—maybe even a lot of them! It helps to remember that a husband is a man, and most men (not all, but most) are not wired for the amount of talking women are capable of. And that's okay!

John Gottman teaches that in order for couples to thrive in their marriages, the vast majority of their interactions need to be positive. He says that in healthy marriages, there is a "magic ratio" of at least five positive interactions for every negative

> *In healthy marriages, there are at least five positive interactions for every negative one.*

one.[7] In Carrie Wrigley's presentation of the 4 T's, she said that if you're trying to heal a very disconnected relationship, you need ten positive interactions for every negative one.

Focusing on the positive doesn't mean that you always overlook or ignore the negative. You are not *ignoring* the negative; you are *intentionally cultivating* the positive! You are increasing the balance in your Emotional Bank Account so that when (not if, but when) the negative needs attention, you can gracefully deal with it or at least rebound quickly.

A New View on the Negative. An interesting point that Carrie taught in her class is that some negative is actually vital in a relationship. Difficult topics such as finances, raising kids, and health concerns need to be addressed. It may be tempting to avoid uncomfortable conversations and ignore things that aren't pleasant to deal with. But confronting and overcoming problems together can strengthen a couple tremendously.

Carrie explained that dealing with difficult issues is like taking out the trash. It may be a not-so-fun chore, but it needs to be done regularly so that the trash doesn't build up and become a huge problem. Finding the right balance in marriage can be a little tricky because couples need to keep their positive interactions high, but they also need to be willing to recognize and address the negative in their marriage. In other words, couples need to "take out the trash" if they want their relationship to flourish.

Avoid Judgment, and Cultivate Understanding. The amount of trash in my marriage decreased significantly when I began applying Rosenberg's principles and techniques of NVC, or Compassionate Communication. NVC helped me avoid judging my husband, and it helped me cultivate a better understanding of his needs and his perspective when we had disagreements.

Rosenberg's goal is to inspire heartfelt connections that allow everyone's needs to be met. He teaches people how to accept themselves and others without judgment. He also teaches them to understand and address their own feelings and needs, and then to connect with the other person's feelings and needs in a way that creates compassion. When this kind of communication happens, conflict and tension are replaced with the desire to support each other. From there, new solutions appear that are more likely to be mutually respectful and satisfying. Even when only one person practices NVC, it helps the couple bridge emotional gaps, and it creates more intimacy in their marriage.

Trust

Trust grows as couples spend time together and talk respectfully and positively *to* each other and *about* each other. One thing my NVC coach stressed about building trust is the importance of being trust*worthy*. She told me I absolutely had to do what I said I would do in every little situation, and when I couldn't, I had to communicate the change as quickly as possible. Why? Because following through builds trust! As I worked to be more communicative and trustworthy, I noticed that the stress levels in my marriage went down and my connection with my husband improved.

In the "honeymoon phase" or early part of a relationship, trust usually comes naturally because of all the positive time and talk the couple enjoys together. But when stress and disappointment find their way into a marriage, it's common for couples to lose that grounding sense of trust. They might even feel betrayed—betrayed by their spouse, by God, by their church, by their family, by anyone who encouraged them to think that marriage was a good idea. This level of disconnection and lack of trust is very painful!

If you don't trust your spouse, or you feel that your spouse doesn't trust you, the 4 T's offer hope. They acknowledge that it's natural not to feel trusting when there's no foundation of positive time and talk, but they also teach that trust can be rebuilt by first focusing on positive time and talk. (Remember that this book isn't for marriages with serious issues like infidelity or abuse. We're talking about two good, faithful, physically safe people here.)

Habitually Turn Toward Each Other

John Gottman says one of the best ways to build trust is to make a habit of turning toward each other rather than away from each other.[8] For example, when your spouse comes into the room and is clearly stressed, you can choose to either turn toward him or her by becoming curious about what's going on, or you can turn away by thinking critical thoughts like, "What's wrong with you now? You're such a stress case. You should just be happy. It's not that hard." Criticism closes you down. Curiosity opens you up.

> *Criticism closes you down. Curiosity opens you up.*

There are many times each day that you can either turn toward or away from your spouse. You can pleasantly say, "Good morning," or you can breeze right by your spouse on your way to the kitchen. You can call or text your spouse sometime during the day or you can make no contact at all. You can greet each other with a smile, a blank face, or a glare. You can ask about each other's day or you can avoid talking. You can eat dinner together or alone. You can spend time together in the evening or go your separate ways. You can talk before bed or you can make sure you're not around at bedtime. And regardless of the time of day, every thought you think about your marriage either turns you toward or away from your spouse.

> *Every thought you think about your marriage either turns you toward or away from your spouse.*

Turning toward each other can include:

- Seeking win-win solutions when you face challenges.
- Being there for each other emotionally.
- Making each other a priority.
- Being sensitive to each other's needs.
- Choosing curiosity over criticism when something bothers one of you.
- Being on time for dates and appointments.
- Coming home when you say you will.
- Following through with what you say you will do.
- Being thoughtful and positive when sharing things about your spouse and your relationship in public.
- Reconnecting through sincere apologies.

Of course, no one has control of what their spouse says or does, but as you focus on turning toward your spouse, you are tipping the domino that has the potential to set in motion a continuous practice of turning toward each other. If you make it a habit to regularly turn toward your spouse, he or she is much more likely to make a habit of turning toward you.

So how do you start turning toward your spouse if you're currently experiencing tension when you're together? Begin by reminding yourself that you and your spouse are two different people with two different backgrounds and lots of different rules and expectations. Then focus on the goodness of your spouse's heart. Choose to focus on the best that is in both of you.

Shortly after I started dating my husband, I realized what an amazing person he is. I sensed it at a deep internal level. I could see it in his eyes and in the way he treated people. His heart is pure and good. I knew it then and I know it now. So when he does something that strikes me as hurtful, I remind myself that no matter how it seems to me as I look through the lens of my background, gender, belief systems, and experiences, *deep down, he never really wants to hurt me.*

Thinking this way helps me stay in a place of trust, and it prevents a lot of unnecessary pain. It helps me get curious about his motive for doing what he did that bothered me. At some point I may choose to ask him what was going on for him when it happened, but usually if I just take some deep breaths and remind myself of his core goodness, I can stay grounded in the love we share.

Since your relationship is uniquely your own, pay close attention to what builds the most trust between you and your spouse, and then do your best to attend to those things. Turning toward your spouse adds to your Emotional Bank Account while increasing the trust in your relationship.

Touch

When the first three T's are in place in a marriage, a couple feels close, connected, and loving. Non-sexual physical affection and sexual intimacy are usually a natural part of their relationship. However, when healthy time, talk, and trust aren't happening, physical touch of any kind becomes less enjoyable. In fact, it can become less and less frequent until there is a dearth of affection and intimacy in the marriage. At that point, neither person feels loved, and neither person feels happy.

It is a sad day for the marriage, but it doesn't have to last forever. Even during the darkest night, there is hope of a bright and beautiful dawn. As the ringmaster in a profound little movie called *Butterfly Circus* says, "The greater the struggle, the more glorious the triumph!" So even if your marital struggles are very difficult right now, your potential for joy is still great. Just by reading this book you are already moving toward that glorious triumph.

When couples are severely disconnected, physical affection and intimacy won't come overnight, nor should they. This is the time to patiently focus on the previous steps in their order and let this final step come naturally.

Touch and Gender Differences

Most men are geared for touch—particularly intimate touch—more so than most women. Engaging in physical intimacy is the way that husbands feel connected to their wives both physically and emotionally. That connection gives them a great amount of enjoyment and makes them feel deeply loved and bonded to their wives. When a husband feels emotionally disconnected from his wife and wants to reconnect, he will most often want to touch her in some way and then escalate that touch into an intimate sexual experience.

HOWEVER . . .

When women feel disconnected, physical touch is usually the last thing they want! A man's natural instinct to touch his wife in order to reconnect will most likely have the exact opposite effect of what he wants. Carrie Wrigley has heard many a woman say that when she feels hurt and disconnected, her husband's touch feels like "acid on her skin."

So what do you do?

Carrie advises men to simply go back to step one and resist the temptation to skip or rush through the first three steps. She says when the steps are rushed, it undermines any progress that's been made, and the relationship will most likely end up in a worse place than before. Sometimes going through the first steps can take only a matter of minutes, but the best approach is to just relax and focus on moving through each step naturally.

Carrie also encourages women to take a step back and approach things from a different perspective. When a husband reaches out wanting an intimate connection it doesn't automatically mean he is trying to use his wife to gratify himself. He's a good man. *He's trying to connect with the woman he chose to spend his life with*. What he's saying is, "I miss you. I want to feel close to you. I love you!"

What Do You Do When You're Not "In the Mood"?

Don't get me wrong. I'm not suggesting that wives should engage in intimate contact every time their husbands reach out to them, or that husbands should engage every time their wives reach out to them. But keep in mind that there are many times when an intimate connection is exactly what a marriage needs in order to thrive. Marriage will bring both spouses greater joy if they understand some basic differences that apply in most situations. Connecting conversation is to most women what sexual intimacy is to most men. Talking is what most women need to feel happily connected, while satisfying sexual intimacy is what most men need to feel happily connected.

So it seems wise to see your spouse's actions in a true perspective. When wives want to talk, they are saying, "I want to connect." When husbands want sexual intimacy, they are also saying, "I want to connect."

Instead of pushing your spouse away when you're not in the mood, check in with yourself and try to understand what you're really feeling. Are you tired, stressed, insecure, overworked? Ask yourself what you might do that would help you feel more relaxed and ready to connect intimately. Do you need to take a few minutes to freshen up? Do you need to shut off all technology and take a shower? Do you need to spend some time together watching a show or having a good chat? Do you need to get your kids playing independently or put them to bed so you have undistracted time for your marriage?

Also, step back and look at your lifestyle in general. Is there anything you need to change to make sure you have the time, energy, and interest necessary to enjoy regular intimacy with your spouse?

A lot of people think sex is just for men, but I strongly disagree. When a wife takes the time to get in the mood for an intimate experience with her husband, *she* benefits greatly. She reconnects with the fact that she's not just a maid, a co-provider, or a mother. She's a woman. And she's the woman her man wants. That feels good! And making her husband feel wanted makes him feel less like a slave, provider, or dad, and more like his woman's man.

Research states that marriages do best when sexual intimacy is scheduled regularly.[9] If possible, I suggest starting with one pre-planned intimate experience per week and then be open to other spontaneous opportunities. If you are willing to experiment and consciously observe your feelings regarding your intimate experiences you will soon discover what really nourishes your connection. Notice how often and what kinds of experiences work best for you and your spouse—fast, slow, fun, chatty, silent, frequent, less frequent, etc. With that knowledge, you can better enjoy your intimate life, while realizing, of course, that from time to time you will need to make adjustments as new situations or changes come into your lives.

If intimacy isn't a comfortable part of your marriage right now, don't stress about it. Just focus on using the 4 T's to build a more enjoyable relationship. As you do so, you will be preparing to experience enjoyable intimacy when your emotional connection has improved. It may not take as long as you think!

PART 2

The Amazing Love Log

HOW TO TAKE YOUR MARRIAGE TO THE NEXT LEVEL

Working briefly on your marriage every day
will do more for your health and longevity
than working out at a health club.
—*John Gottman*[10]

Don't carry your mistakes around with you.
Instead, place them under your feet
and use them as stepping stones.
Never regret.
If it's good, it's wonderful.
If it's bad, it's experience.
—*Anonymous*

How the Love Log Came to Be

The Love Log is a tracking tool that will help you learn how to nurture your marriage. It has brought about remarkable changes in some very challenging relationships. Let me explain a little about how the Love Log came to be.

A few years ago I started working with a wonderful health coach named Sarah Klein. Although I had been exercising and eating well since I was a teenager, I still didn't feel very healthy or energetic. In fact, I felt tired and grumpy almost every day. I had also suffered from a painful, chronic digestive problem for over a decade.

The first thing Sarah did was give me a tiny notebook with a simple format for tracking. She told me to spend five minutes a night recording everything I had eaten that day, how I felt right after I'd eaten it, and how I felt several hours later. She also told me to write down things I felt grateful for that day.

It was such a doable plan that despite feeling overwhelmed with life, I actually wanted to give the process a try. If the notebook had been any bigger or the format any more complex, I'm sure I wouldn't have done it consistently. But, even as tired as I was each night, I could still manage five minutes of focused note writing at the end of the day. I even decided to add another category and track how much exercise I was getting each day.

Once I started keeping that health journal, it only took me a few weeks to discover some patterns. For instance, when I ate milk products, I felt sluggish and my stomach hurt. When I ate cucumbers, I felt light and energized. My tracking helped me realize I wasn't exercising as much as I had thought I was. I also noticed that writing about things I was grateful for elevated my mood significantly.

After I nailed down which foods I needed to avoid and which ones consistently made me feel great, I used the journaling technique to determine how much sleep I needed to feel my best during the day. Throughout the whole process, I kept observing how different things affected my digestive problems, and I was ecstatic when that pain finally resolved itself. Once I felt confident in my daily health habits, I set my little notebook aside.

It was sometime later that I decided I wanted to improve my connection with my husband. I was curious to know what we could regularly do that would really nurture our marriage. Because the nightly tracking had been so helpful with my health issues, I decided to try it with my relationship.

I bought another tiny notebook, designed a simple daily format, and wrote out what I planned to do with my husband each day for the following week. Every night I spent a few minutes writing down what we had done that day, how I felt about it, and how close our relationship felt. I also wrote down things I felt particularly grateful for during the day, and any positive experiences we had enjoyed together.

After just a few weeks of tracking, I was able to identify things I wanted to continue doing and things I wanted to change. I experimented and played with new ideas while also noting things we were already doing that worked well. Whether I was observing something we did naturally or whether I was trying a new experiment, I paid close attention to how I felt during our interactions and made notes about my feelings.

Within a couple of months, my husband and I were smiling at each other more often, we were talking more, we teased more, we spent more happy time together, we were better friends, and we were more physically affectionate. It was then that it dawned on me that I was actually living my version of *happily ever after*.

When I looked back and realized just how much that little notebook had helped me in my efforts to improve my marriage, I began to call it my Love Log.

Setting Yourself Up for Success

Three things will set you up for success in using a Love Log to improve your marriage: attitude, "mindset mantras," and self-care.

Attitude

How do you feel about your marriage right now? Do you feel excited, interested, or curious to discover what will enhance your relationship? Do you feel stressed and believe there's something seriously wrong with your marriage that needs to be fixed right away? Are you somewhere in between? Wherever you are is a great place to begin!

If you're excited and curious, you are on the right track! You've got the attitude for success.

If you're feeling stressed, there's probably a very good reason. Just try to open your mind to the hope of positive change. When stress is your overriding feeling, it will have a tendency to block the good things the Love Log has to offer you. So, take some deep breaths, say a quick prayer, and remind yourself that you and your husband are both good people doing the best you can.

Even in the face of some very difficult challenges, many other couples have bridged a significant emotional gap and are now enjoying happier marriages than they had ever dreamed possible. You can too.

Mindset Mantras

A mantra is a word or phrase that is repeated with the intention of quieting the mind and cultivating something a person wants to create in his or her life. Mantras are very helpful in maintaining a positive mindset, and a positive mindset is essential to your success in creating a happier marriage. I recommend that you come up with two default mantras: one to cultivate a positive mindset and the other to stop negative thoughts. Mantras are simple and to the point. You can adjust or change them as you go along, so don't worry about getting them perfect from the beginning.

Here are some examples of mantras that cultivate a positive marriage mindset. The first three might work best for people who are very disconnected, and the others could work well for people who are looking to go from good to great.

- We can figure this out. It is okay to be right where we are.
- Other people with worse challenges have worked out their differences. We can too.
- Even though it's been rough, I know we are committed to each other and we'll get through this.
- More and more love and connection are coming our way.
- I'm grateful for the practical ideas that come to me about how we can grow closer together.

- I'm so thankful for all my spouse gives to me and to our family.
- Marriage is awesome!
- Marriage is fun!
- I love you and you love me, and life's as good as it can be!

Here are examples of mantras that could be used to stop negative thoughts and focus the mind on the positive:

- No matter what it looks like to me, deep down my husband (or wife) never intends to hurt me.
- I'm sure there's a reason why he (or she) did that, even if it doesn't make sense to me right now.
- We're both doing the best we can.
- It's okay to hit a bump. We'll get back on track soon.
- It must be time for more "deposits" because I'm sure that wouldn't have bothered me if we felt closer to each other.

When I catch myself thinking a negative thought, I have learned to stop myself and repeat my mantra. Then I say a quick prayer and intentionally distract myself. When I'm feeling better, I can revisit whatever bothered me. Usually, the negative feelings of the moment have dissipated, and I just need to focus on cultivating the positive again. If I still feel we need to resolve something, my thoughts are clearer and I can approach the situation (and my husband) from a more loving perspective.

Self-Care

You may define yourself by one of your many roles: husband or wife, parent, provider, homemaker, or your title at work, but at the core of any role, you are still an individual. You are unique and beautiful just as you are. And the better you care for yourself, the better "self" you bring to your marriage as well as everything else in your life.

So let's take a moment to check in on your personal needs.

- Are you getting enough sleep? Seven to eight hours a night is a typical range for adults.

- Are you getting enough water? Health experts recommend drinking half your body weight in ounces each day.

- Are you eating primarily healthy, whole foods including a good balance of fruits, vegetables, whole grains, and protein?

- Are you regularly enjoying exercise that makes you feel great?

- Are you spending time with friends who uplift, support, and inspire you and who strengthen your positive thoughts about yourself, your spouse, and your marriage?

- Are you managing your stress well? Do you have a variety of ways to successfully reduce your stress level when you notice it rising?

- Are you taking time to get dressed and ready for the day so you feel good about how you look?

- Are there other things you do or could do to proactively care for yourself as an individual?

If you're already taking good care of yourself, that's excellent! Keep it up! If not, start small. Pick one or two things to work on, and then add others when you feel you can handle more. Notice how caring for yourself affects your marriage and other areas of your life.

Personalizing Your Love Log

This is *your* Love Log so you can make it look as simple or as fancy as you'd like. When I started, I just bought a tiny notebook with a nice cover and blank pages. Sometimes I enjoy writing with colorful gel pens, but that's about as fancy as I get. Some people like to personalize their notebooks by writing their mantras in the front, or decorating it with stickers, or drawing in it. Do whatever makes your Love Log feel positive and special to you.

Red Cars and Orange Butterflies

I have a friend who could be a happiness expert. She cultivates her own happiness daily and spreads happiness wherever she goes. One day I asked about her daily happiness habits and she recommended a little book called *E^2: Nine Do-It-Yourself Energy Experiments That Prove Your Thoughts Create Your Reality* by Pam Grout.

My friend said that I might not always enjoy the way Pam expresses her ideas, but she said that the experiments were definitely worth doing.

In the book, Pam claims that we miss a lot of amazing things in our lives because we're not actively looking for them. She invites readers to do a couple of simple experiments that she said would prove this. The first experiment involves counting cars, so one Sunday morning I decided to count all the red cars I saw throughout the day. Since the only driving I planned to do was the few miles to church and back, I expected to see about five red cars.

Right away, though, I noticed a pile of toy cars that our youngest daughter likes to play with. Since I hadn't specified that the cars had to be full-sized, functioning red cars, I decided I would count toy cars, too. By the time I headed out the door, I'd already counted more than five red cars.

On the way to church I recruited my family to help me. They excitedly pointed out several red cars that I surely would have missed if I'd been counting on my own.

After lunch we decided to go for a drive, and by the time we got home, we were up to 117 red cars. Then I remembered a potluck dinner I had been invited to that evening. On the drive to and from the dinner, I scoured the countryside for all the red cars I could find. When I got home that night, I had counted over 200 red cars throughout the day—a far cry from the five red cars I had expected to see!

The next experiment Pam suggests is similar, but this time she says to count butterflies. I chose to count orange butterflies because I *love* orange butterflies. However, it was October and the weather had already turned cold, so I truly thought I wouldn't see a single living butterfly, orange or otherwise. I had no plans to go to town the next day so I knew I wouldn't be seeing a lot of clothing or products that might have orange butterflies on them. All in all, I went to bed that night thinking I probably wouldn't see a single orange butterfly, but I planned to keep my eyes open just in case.

As I was getting dressed the next morning, my jaw almost hit the floor! My favorite pair of jeans that I was putting on had an orange butterfly stitched onto them! And when I went to make my bed, I noticed the wall poster I'd colored the year before. There were many butterflies on the poster, and *eleven* of them were orange. On a day that I thought I'd see zero orange butterflies, I counted twelve before I'd even left my bedroom!

I stopped counting at ten o'clock that morning after having counted 130 orange butterflies. Most of them were on fabrics and in pictures, but the last one I counted was indeed a living, breathing butterfly that fluttered across my path as I was walking home from my neighbor's house.

So, what do red cars and orange butterflies have to do with your marriage? Actually, everything! Just as I easily found way more red cars and orange butterflies than I had ever imagined, there were many, many good things going on in my marriage that I didn't notice simply because I wasn't looking for them.

Could the same thing be happening to you?

Try your own experiment. Try watching for all the wonderful "red cars and orange butterflies" in your marriage that you might be overlooking. Write down all the things your spouse does that you're grateful for, things your spouse thanks you for, things you like about him (or her), things you like about your marriage, things you like about your lifestyle, things you already do that connect you and your spouse. Also write down positive experiences that you and your spouse enjoy together.

Keep your list handy and add anything positive that comes to mind for a few days. You might want to write your list in the back of this book or on the first pages of your Love Log. Let gratitude completely saturate your mind for a few minutes each day. Marriages thrive on gratitude and appreciation, so this is a great place to start building your *happily ever after*.

Keeping Your Experiments Confidential

Keeping a Love Log is a personal process. Your observations, experiments, and notes are designed to help you gather the information you need to understand how you can strengthen and enrich your marriage. I strongly recommend that you *do not* discuss what you're doing with your spouse because it will affect your experiments and you won't get accurate results. (If you happen to be reading this book as a couple, you can decide together how you want to approach sharing your experiments, results, and things you're grateful for. Just make sure that what you do brings you closer together.)

Also, be very careful about sharing what you're doing with others. Your marriage is sacred and must be treated with love and respect if you want it to improve. Your spouse will almost certainly feel betrayed if he or she finds out that a lot of people know you are "working on your marriage" without his or her knowledge.

Having said that, many people—especially women—can benefit from talking with a competent counselor or a trusted friend. However, you need to be very selective about who you let into your confidence. You aren't looking for someone to take sides or to sympathize with you about the difficulty of your situation. You're looking for someone who will wisely support you when you feel frustrated, and who will enthusiastically celebrate your successes with you.

There are times when asking your parents or a sibling for guidance regarding a problem in your marriage is wise and warranted, but for this experience, your best choice is probably going to be someone who doesn't even know your spouse. However, if you don't have another good option, you may want to consider someone who knows and loves you both. No matter who you choose, the person should have total faith in you and in your marriage.

When I first started keeping my Love Log, I didn't talk to anyone but God. He's great at keeping everything confidential! It helped me tremendously to take time to pray *and listen* for guidance. Although having a human confidante can be very helpful, I sincerely hope you will regularly spend some time talking to God and listening for His guidance.

What to Record in Your Love Log

The purpose of your Love Log is to help you determine what things consistently connect you and your spouse so you can strengthen your marriage by repeating them.

This is what the two facing pages of a blank Love Log look like:

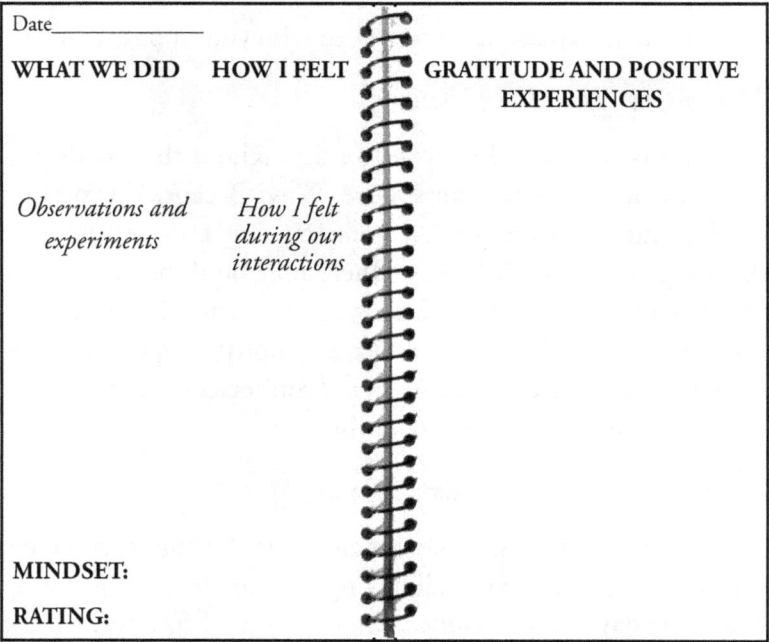

On the left hand pages, you will record:

- **Observations** of things you (or your spouse) already do that contribute to your connection or disconnection and how you feel during that time.
- **Experiments** you intentionally tried, their results, how you felt during your experiment, and whether or not the things you tried helped you feel closer to your spouse.
- How you worked with your thoughts to cultivate a positive **mindset** and stop negative thinking.
- An overall daily connection **rating** of how close you felt to your spouse that day on a scale of 0–10.

On the right hand pages you will record:

- Things you're **grateful** for about your marriage.
- **Positive experiences** you shared with your spouse that day.

More on the "How I Felt" Section

It's important to note how you feel throughout the day during your interactions with your spouse. Why? Because this process is all about discovering what connects you as a couple, and that's a perception—a feeling. There may be things you think *should* connect you, but when you pay attention and take notes, you will realize that they actually don't! That's why you're tracking—to see what makes you *feel* connected—so make sure you fill in the "How I Felt" column.

More on Your Daily Connection Rating

I use a 0–10 rating scale where 0 is feeling completely disconnected and 10 is totally living my *happily ever after*. Any particular day could include a wide variety of feelings, so just look back on the day and see how you feel about your overall marriage connection. A day that has been pretty smooth may get the same rating as a day that was rough, but ended with a strong feeling of connection. The ratings give you a quick overview of how connected you felt during a specific period of time, such as a few weeks or a month.

A Day in the Life of a Love Log

On the next page is an example of one day in the life of a Love Log. You'll see how all the sections fit in just two pages and how simple and easy the format really is.

Example of the Love Log Pages for One Day

Date _____

WHAT WE DID	**HOW I FELT**
AM: *Snuggled & chatted*	*Great*
Walked the kids to school	*Happy*
Talked before work	*Stressed, bad timing*
Called him during my lunchtime	*Stressful! It wasn't his lunchtime so he couldn't focus.*
PM: *Kissed & hugged when we saw each other after work*	*Great!*
Took a quick walk & held hands	*So nice*

MINDSET: *Great job. I stopped a negative spiral when our phone call went bad.*

RATING: 7

Based on the notes taken for this particular day, I might:

- Watch for the opportunity to have another morning snuggle sometime soon.
- Try taking another walk soon to see if it feels as connecting as it did on this day.
- Try avoiding a long conversation right when he's walking out the door for work.

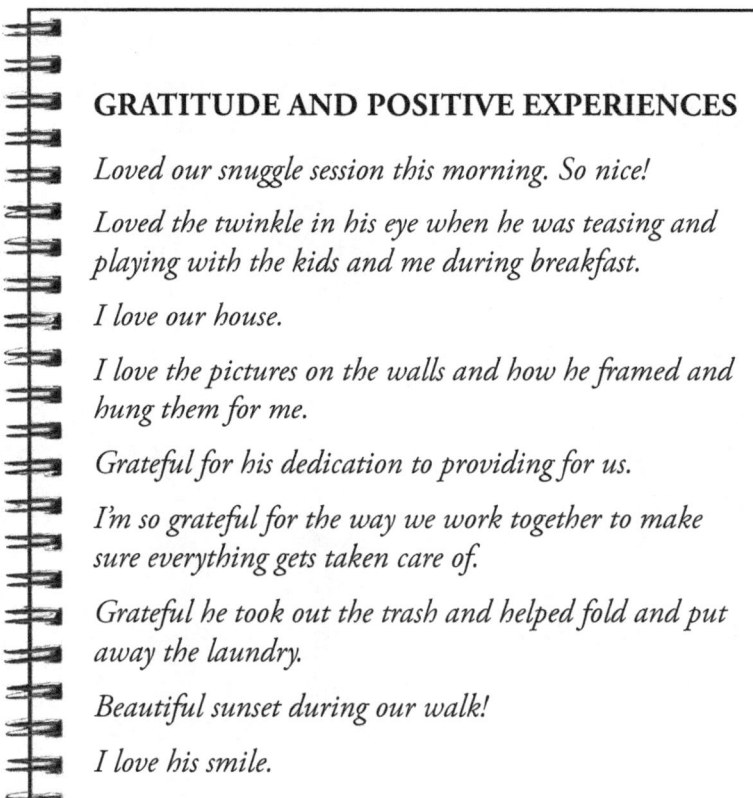

GRATITUDE AND POSITIVE EXPERIENCES

Loved our snuggle session this morning. So nice!

Loved the twinkle in his eye when he was teasing and playing with the kids and me during breakfast.

I love our house.

I love the pictures on the walls and how he framed and hung them for me.

Grateful for his dedication to providing for us.

I'm so grateful for the way we work together to make sure everything gets taken care of.

Grateful he took out the trash and helped fold and put away the laundry.

Beautiful sunset during our walk!

I love his smile.

- Make a note not to call him at lunchtime.
- Ask him to call as he's leaving work so I know when he'll be home.
- Write a "thank you" note telling him how much I appreciated his help with the trash and laundry today.
- Try talking at night before bed.

Designing Your Daily Connection Plan

Creating and following a Daily Connection Plan is a great way to improve your marriage. The first step in designing your Daily Connection Plan is to brainstorm and write down any ideas you might want to try. You can use the 4 T's as a guide when choosing your experiments.

The best ideas are practical, repeatable, and potentially-connecting activities that are short, inexpensive, and varied. For example, you might enjoy taking a short walk, rubbing your spouse's feet or shoulders, watching a short TV show, having a special treat in the morning or at night, dancing in the living room, or reading a book together. What else comes to mind that you could try? Jot everything down. (In Appendix A, you will find a rating scale that will help you determine where to start.)

After you brainstorm, select the things you'd like to try during your first week and write them down in calendar form on the back of your brainstorming paper, on a sticky note, in your Love Log, or on some other paper you can keep handy.

Your Daily Connection Plan could look something like this:

Sun.	Mon.	Tues.	Wed.	Thurs.	Fri.	Sat.
Planning and talk time	Read together	Foot rub	Snuggle or intimate time	Watch TV together	Take a walk together	Out to dinner
30–60 min.	15 min.	15 min.	30+ min.	30 min.	15 min.	2 hrs.

As you can see, this sample plan has 15–30 minute ideas for weekdays, and longer ones for Saturday and Sunday.

Earlier I suggested a pre-planned weekly time for intimate bonding, which you see scheduled in the plan for Wednesday. I also highly recommend scheduling a weekly planning and talk time. Life is *so* busy, and often spouses feel like they are running parallel lives, hardly knowing what's going on in the other person's world. The weekly planning and talk time helps couples feel connected and provides the first two T's—*time* and *talk*—in one setting.

My husband and I currently have a Sunday chat that opens communication for the rest of the week. We've done it in a variety of ways over the past six years and it's like magic for us. It helps us reconnect with each other in a way that nothing else does. We get an overview of what's going on in each other's lives, how we're each feeling, and how we can support each other. (In Appendix B, you will find specific details on the weekly planning and talk time.)

Whatever you do, make sure your Daily Connection Plan is practical for *you*. The goal is to design a plan that is repeatable, enjoyable, and connecting. When you think of it, it should make you smile. It should make you feel confident and happy.

If you're excited about your plan, your spouse will most likely jump on board, especially if you only plan short activities that can easily fit into your day.

If it stresses you out to do different activities throughout the week, focus on finding one activity you can do every day that consistently connects you. Some couples I know like to read a book together at night. Others take a walk every evening. Others share a specific snack every night. It's all about connection, regardless of the activity you're doing. So if you like variety, build in variety. If you like to do the same thing daily, make that your plan. This is your marriage. Figure out what works for you and have fun doing it!

Be a Scientist

As you begin experimenting and tracking your results, keep two things in mind:

1. You're just experimenting.
2. *All* feedback is valuable!

Good scientists approach their experimentation with curiosity. They may have an idea of what to expect, but they're not attached to a certain result. They just closely observe the experiment and record whatever results they get. Then they study their results and decide what might be a good experiment to try next.

You are the scientist here, and this is a *no-pressure* process. If you try something and you love the results, great! If you try something and you don't like the results, that's also great! It's all good feedback! Just use your Love Log to record whatever you tried and how you felt about it. This will help you decide what to try next.

A quotation from the book, *Change Anything*, sums this up nicely.

> Be the scientist and the subject. . . . Write down your plan. . . . Then learn what's working and what isn't, and make adjustments. If you keep a record of your evolving plan, you'll make new mistakes rather than repeating the old ones.[11]

A Note about Flexibility

Don't worry if something you planned doesn't fit into your day, especially if you and your spouse are already doing something that is particularly connecting. Just enjoy the moment.

There will also be times when your plan needs to be set aside because one of you is sick or has had a really rough day. Just make a few notes about what you did and how you felt, or note that you didn't do anything that day and explain why. Then get back on track the next day.

Reviewing and Adjusting Your Plan

After your first week of experimenting and tracking, review your Love Log and make a new plan for the following week. Schedule the things you want to do again and select new things from your brainstorming list that you would like to try. After you repeat this process for three or four weeks you will most likely have a pretty solid Daily Connection Plan in place that you can enjoy for many weeks to come. If after a while you decide you want a change, adjust your activities to keep your marriage interesting and fun.

What about Making Monthly and Yearly Plans?

Monthly and yearly plans can be a bonus for those who want to make them, but the reality is, if you're unhappy and disconnected on a daily basis, a big activity or vacation won't bridge the emotional gap in your marriage. A happy marriage requires daily nurturing, not just a monthly or yearly booster shot.

Would you ever go to an all-you-can-eat buffet, completely stuff yourself, and then expect not to eat again for another month? Of course not. Your body doesn't work that way, and neither does your marriage. So focus on the Daily Connection Plan, and then whenever you do decide to throw in a larger activity, you'll have the foundation of a great friendship so you can more fully enjoy it.

I'll never forget a conversation with a man I met a few years ago when I was traveling with my mom to Philadelphia. I sat on the plane watching people drag their luggage down the aisle, wondering which of them would be taking the empty seat beside us. When I saw this man approaching, I noticed the light in his eyes and the positive energy he exuded. When he got to our row, he put his bag in a nearby overhead bin, carefully squeezed in front of us, and sat down in the empty window seat.

He introduced himself immediately and began talking to us. The plane had barely left the ground when the topic turned to marriage and family. He spoke so passionately about the importance of marriage that I asked him if he was a marriage therapist or a motivational speaker or something. He laughed and said no, but that marriage was something he cared about deeply.

I figured that someone with that much passion would have a fantastic relationship and that I could learn a ton from him, but when I asked about his marriage, his face fell. He explained that he and his wife were both working a lot of long hours and that they were no longer close at all. He said he deeply loved and admired her, and that he absolutely adored his kids, but because he traveled so much for his work, he didn't spend as much time with his family as he wanted to.

He brightened as he told us about a big vacation they planned to go on in a few months, but then his face fell again as he admitted that he knew a long, expensive vacation would never compensate for all the time and connection he missed with them on a daily basis. It was one of the most profound things I learned from him that day.

> *"You can't put your marriage on cruise control."*

Another thing he said that stuck with me was, "You can't put your marriage on cruise control." He went on to explain that he had learned—hopefully not too late—that you can't ignore your marriage and think it will be fine while you focus on your career and other things in life.

A marriage needs daily attention to stay strong and healthy. The comparison between a marriage and a plant is another metaphor that really resonates with me. They are both alive, and they both need continual nourishment to thrive. You will notice that I said continual nourishment, not constant nourishment. They may seem similar, but they are not the same thing. I love how the following quotation from Carrie Wrigley's website explains the difference.

> You don't have to flood a potted flower to keep it alive and vibrant. You don't have to change the oil in your car every day to keep it running smoothly. And you don't have give your spouse 100% of your time and attention every day. But give 100% of your focus and attention for at least part of every day. . . . Protect your marriage—cultivate and nourish it intentionally—and it can remain strong, joyful, and unified.[12]

Protect your marriage—cultivate and nourish it intentionally—and it can remain strong, joyful, and unified.

When I was a child, one of my mother's best friends was married to a very successful salesman. Almost every month he won an award in his company for closing the most business deals. He devoted his whole life to his work, so he was rarely home. But he tried to make up for his absence by periodically giving her an expensive gift, such as a leaded glass China hutch, a grand piano, a new car, or an impressive vacation. She became more and more frustrated and told him repeatedly that fancy things could never make up for his being gone all the time. Not surprisingly, they eventually divorced.

A few years later, my mother's friend married again, this time to a schoolteacher. There were no more expensive gifts or vacations, but her new husband understood the importance of building their marriage on a solid emotional foundation. He offered their relationship continual nourishment, and it quickly blossomed into a beautiful *happily ever after* for both of them. They have continued to nourish their relationship, and today, after almost thirty years of marriage, they are enjoying their *happily ever after* more than ever.

Recently I read on the Internet about a "save-cation," which is a term for a big vacation a couple goes on to try to save their marriage. According to the examples cited, a save-cation actually did bring a few couples back together, but more often than not, the save-cation didn't accomplish its purpose. Why? Because emotional intimacy is built on a foundation of many little, pleasant daily connections.

So am I suggesting that you shouldn't go on vacations? Not at all. Enjoy your vacations and make as many wonderful memories as you can. Just don't fool yourself into thinking that an extravagant vacation will make up for a lack of consistent daily connection. All the vacations in the world can't nourish a marriage like loving, daily connections do.

Customizing Your Love Log

As you use your Love Log, you may find that you want to add to or change the format a little. One woman I worked with started recording the time she went to bed because she wondered if her late night schedule was hurting her relationship. Another included what she ate throughout the day because she suspected that her diet was influencing her attitude. In both cases, their tracking showed them definitively that those particular behaviors did indeed affect their marriages. Customizing their Love Logs also helped them stay on track as they developed new habits that improved their relationships.

For a time, I included notes in my Love Log about my eating habits and my spiritual practice. I discovered that when I was eating well, I was able to pay more attention to my husband because my energy was high and my body felt good. My tracking also helped me see that a consistent spiritual practice enhanced my marriage relationship significantly. At the time, I would ask God in the morning what was the most important thing that I could do that day to bless my marriage. I would wait for an answer, write down what came to me, and then make that my number one priority for the day. It worked wonders for my marriage!

As I mentioned earlier, tracking what I do shows me exactly how well I follow through with my good intentions. Often, I *think* I'm doing something consistently, but when I track it, I find I'm doing it much less than I thought, like when I started tracking how much I was exercising. Tracking brings greater awareness and helps me prioritize things that have a positive effect on my life.

So, take a few minutes and think about it. Is there anything that might be affecting your mental, physical, or emotional health? Try tracking it in your Love Log for a while to see if you're right. Once you have a written daily record of how things are actually going, you may decide you want to make some adjustments and track the new results in your Love Log. Customize it in whatever way you feel will be most beneficial.

However, if you do decide you want to track a few extra things in your Love Log, just be sure to keep it simple. My rule is that if my notes don't fit on those two little pages, I'm writing too much. Your daily tracking should only take about five minutes. If you find you really want to write more, do it in a regular journal.

How to Quickly Reconnect When One of You Loses It

Everybody has triggers, hot spots, or buttons that will get pushed. I have them. You have them. Your spouse has them. Your friends and neighbors have them. So just expect that hot buttons will get pushed, and make it a part of your experimentation process to learn how to get back on track quickly.

Of course, the best thing to do is to prevent triggering as much as possible. Try to notice the first signs that your stress levels are escalating and stop yourself, take some deep breaths, and use your mantras. You may need to give yourself a time out by leaving the room for a few minutes. If quick and simple things like that don't work and you're definitely triggered—meaning your stress levels are so high that you feel furious and irrational—give yourself some space as quickly as you can. Nothing you say or do is going to be constructive when you are that upset.

Gottman calls this state of stress "flooding."[13] Your brain and body are literally flooded with stress hormones, and he says it takes at least twenty minutes to get your body to reset. He suggests doing something distracting or calming rather than calling your best friend and ranting about why you're angry since that will only feed the problem. So, do some exercise, watch a show, read a book, or work on a project. But then what?

I highly recommend using your Love Log to track your experiences and feelings when it comes to triggering. Learning what triggers you and your spouse, as well as how you can best respond when one of you is triggered, is very useful information! So when something negative happens, notice what triggered you or your spouse. Write what you did to prevent triggering. Write what you did to recover after one of you flooded, and note how it worked.

> *Learning what triggers you and your spouse, as well as how you can best respond when one of you is triggered, is very useful information!*

Harness the power of prayer by asking God, "How can we quickly get back on track?" and follow the guidance you receive. Try saying, "I'm sorry." Try writing a note. Try saying nothing and just going back to the 4 T's. Try getting frustrated. Try staying calm. Track what you try and how it worked, so you can figure out how to quickly make up and move on both this time and in the future.

How Long Will It Take to See Results?

When you begin using a Love Log and applying the 4 T's in your marriage, you will probably notice positive results rather quickly. However, the time it will take you to get to a place of *happily ever after* will depend on where your relationship is when you begin experimenting, and how persistent you are in your efforts.

As you watch for results, it's always good to keep in mind that *you are only in control of yourself.* This book helps you understand how you can offer opportunities to draw closer together as a couple, but you don't get to decide what your spouse does with those opportunities. Viewing this process as an interesting and fun experiment helps you avoid disappointment, and it allows you to accept the pace that is needed to rebuild and strengthen your relationship.

Sometimes you may feel like you are making great progress. Other times you may feel like things have totally regressed. During the times when you feel like you're going backwards, take a time out for some self-care, do your best to fill your heart with gratitude, and hold on to your hope and your vision of a happy marriage. You and your spouse are two good people, with different backgrounds, genetics, temperaments, etc.

Meshing these differences can be difficult at times no matter how long you've been married.

Talk to God. Talk to a trusted friend. If you really can't seem to get back into a positive mindset, talk to a good counselor or contact me on my website and let's see what we can do to help you get back on track.

Here's the thing: For most people, books don't change lives. *Applying what's in the book* is what changes lives. Keeping on track, especially at first, can be a real challenge.

In past years, whenever I came across powerful ideas and suggestions that I knew had the potential to be life changing, I'd get super excited and make a plan for applying the new ideas in my life. But then I'd get distracted and those great ideas and actions would slip through the cracks. Weeks or months later, I'd look back and realize that I hadn't been successful in changing my habits at all! How frustrating!

It wasn't until I started working with coaches that real, lasting change started happening. My health coach and my NVC coach provided me with wonderful support as I was making changes in my health practices and my marriage relationship. Their insights and encouragement carried me through some challenging times when I felt really discouraged.

If you would like some extended support as you begin using The 4 T's of Relationship Building or as you begin to experiment with your Love Log, I invite you to check out the programs available on my website. They are designed to help you transform the "high" of those initial good intentions into lasting changes that will enrich your life and increase the happiness in your marriage.

CONCLUSION

Celebrate Your Marriage!

Your marriage is one of a kind. Celebrate it! Have fun!

Have faith that you can figure things out.

Take a step back when you need to.

Turn toward each other.

Look for rewarding win-win solutions.

Pray.

Surround yourself with happily married people.

Work your Daily Connection Plan and fall back in love again and again and again.

Here's to your version of *happily ever after!*

Appendix A

Using a Rating Scale to Determine How to Proceed

This section is designed to give you a more specific idea of where your marriage is right now and how you might most effectively proceed. Begin by rating how close you have felt to your spouse over the past month on a scale of 0–10 with 0 being not close at all and 10 being totally connected.

Rating	Relationship
0–2	*Completely disconnected.* Feel agitated, apathetic, awkward, or unpleasant when together.
3–5	*Somewhat connected.* Feel connected sometimes, but the relationship is still rough much of the time.
6–7	*Very connected.* Feel connected most of the time, but there's still room for improvement.
8–10	*Fully connected.* Both enjoy time together, respect each other, seek win-win solutions, connect regularly, and reconnect as needed.

Now that you've got your rating, read through the sections below for suggestions on how to proceed. Realize that overlap in each stage in common. For example, if you're currently rating your relationship at a 0-2, you will likely be talking and touching at times, but your *focus to improve your relationship* will just be practicing your mindset mantras and getting to where you're comfortable in the same room together for fifteen minutes at a time.

RATING: 0–2
GOAL: *Be in the same room more comfortably.*

I'm sorry you're feeling so disconnected! I applaud you for staying together and wanting to work things out!

At this stage, don't try to fix your marriage or your spouse by attempting to talk things out. When the marriage is this stressed, experts recommend backing off on the marriage focus and taking some time to nurture yourself as an individual.[14]

Don't expect overnight changes to occur. You likely have a history of hurt, and your Emotional Bank Account is way overdrawn. It will take time to forgive and rebuild trust. That's okay. Remind yourself that other couples have been where you are now and they've been able to successfully rebuild happy marriages. You can do it too.

Your main focus needs to be cultivating a positive mindset. Create your mantras and use them daily. Diligently look for anything in your marriage and about your spouse that you can feel grateful for, and pay attention to any positive experiences. Write those things in your Love Log. If you are having a really hard time finding anything positive about your marriage or your spouse, you can write about things outside of your marriage as well.

Work on spending short amounts of time (15 minutes or less) in the same room *while radiating positive thoughts and feelings.* Make observations of things you do that connect or disconnect you. You won't want to experiment with too many things yet. Just get to the point where you can be in the same space together fairly comfortably.

If you'd like to design a Daily Connection Plan, give it a shot, but keep *all* activities very short. If you don't feel like doing one yet, don't force it.

RATING: 3–5
GOAL: *Get to where you want to talk more and start working on a Daily Connection Plan.*

You're probably in a state of negative sentiment override. You have more negative than positive interactions, and your Emotional Bank Account balance is either low or overdrawn. Apply the suggestions for those who rated their connection at a 0–2 until you start wanting to talk more. At that point, fill your conversations with positive things as much as possible, doing your best to always be authentic. Also, try to listen attentively and be understanding if your spouse needs to vent. Gottman says the "magic ratio" for positive to negative interactions in healthy marriages is 5 to 1.[15] Carrie Wrigley said if you're healing a relationship, the ratio needs to go up to 10 to 1.

If you haven't designed a Daily Connection Plan to experiment with yet, you are probably ready to try that now. So write down a variety of practical activities you want to try and plan which activities you will try on each day of the upcoming week. Remember to be the scientist and view your results without judgment so you can have fun with your experimenting.

Rating: 6–7

Goal: *Create a Daily Connection Plan that will bump you up to the next level.*

You are in a state of positive sentiment override most of the time. That's wonderful!

So now you're comfortable in the same room together, talking openly, and working on keeping 5–10 positive interactions for every negative one. Now it's time to focus on building trust in your relationship.

First, think about what you already know about the things that matter most to you and your spouse when it comes to building trust. Is it vital to you that you know exactly what time your spouse will be home? Does your spouse get triggered when you share things about your relationship in public? Review the trust section in the How Relationships are Built chapter to see if any other ideas come to mind. If you're open to it, ask your spouse what matters most to him or her and share what matters most to you, then start working on respecting those preferences on a daily basis. This is an investment of time and energy that will yield great results in your marriage.

Besides focusing on building trust, revisit your Daily Connection Plan. Based on your results so far, adjust your activities and keep experimenting and adjusting until you feel confident that you have a practical plan for nurturing your marriage on a daily basis.

Rating: 8–10

Goal: *Keep doing what works best for you. As needed, adjust your Daily Connection Plan to keep your relationship fresh and fun.*

When you rate your connection this high, your main focus is to enjoy working your Daily Connection Plan. Keep an eye on your mindset and keep cultivating positivity. When things happen that bring stress into your lives, turn toward each other, find win-win solutions, and quickly reconnect. Keep nourishing your marriage every day. Adjust your activities when you need something new to keep your relationship fresh.

Also, share what you're doing! One way you can do this while honoring the privacy of your marriage is by emailing me your experiences so that I can pass them on to others anonymously. Or you can post something through my social media sites in a way that feels comfortable to you and your spouse. Either way, celebrating what's working for you not only inspires and supports others, it also reinforces your desire to keep nurturing your own marriage.

When you're feeling totally connected and on a roll, it's time to revisit your nightly note-taking process. If you want to continue as you have been, do so for as long as it benefits you. If you want to shift your focus to another area like health or spirituality, go for it! Regardless of whether or not you shift focus, I highly recommend continuing some kind of gratitude-and-positive-experience journaling as a way to cultivate happiness in your life.

Below is the original rating table along with suggestions for each stage for easy reference.

Rating	Relationship	Main Focus
0–2	*Completely disconnected.* Feel agitated, apathetic, awkward, or unpleasant when together.	*Time.* Manage negative thoughts, nurture positive thoughts, and practice mindset mantras.
3–5	*Somewhat connected.* Feel connected sometimes, but the relationship is still rough much of the time.	*Talk.* Keep nurturing positive thoughts. Work on hitting the magic ratio of 5 to 1 or, better yet, 10 to 1.
6–7	*Very connected.* Feel connected most of the time, but there's still room for improvement.	*Trust.* Keep watching thoughts and working on the magic ratio. Build trust in ways that matter most to you and your spouse.
8–10	*Fully connected.* Both enjoy time together, respect each other, seek win-win solutions, connect regularly, and reconnect as needed.	*Touch.* Keep thoughts positive. Keep the magic ratio going. Reinforce trust. Enjoy non-sexual and sexual affection often.

Appendix B

How to Get the Best Mileage Out of Your Weekly Planning and Talk Time

As you know, I highly recommend a weekly planning and talk time—preferably on Sunday—as you look toward your upcoming week. This starts out your week with the first two T's: *time* and *talk*.

My husband and I started this tradition over six years ago in an attempt to connect in a positive way and to resolve things that bothered us throughout the previous week. It was a pre-planned "take out the trash" time.

For over a year, we used a specific agenda, which I have included below—and yes, we usually went through the whole thing. One rule we had was to start with the positive and really focus on that. Then when we got to the potentially touchy issues, we had already put some deposits in our Emotional Bank Accounts so we felt less like opponents and more like a team.

After a year, we felt more connected on a daily basis so we started to relax on the agenda and just think of things we wanted to talk about. We'd share what was going on in our upcoming week, talk about how the kids were doing, talk about our goals, and bring up any issues we needed to resolve. Now I just start the conversation with "So, what's going on for you this week?" and off we go.

I like to set aside an hour, but we stop when we don't have anything else to say or when I see my husband's eyes start to glaze over, whichever comes first. Sometimes it only takes 15 minutes, but other times it takes the full hour. Sometimes we get through our regular stuff and then talk about something totally different, which often ends up taking the rest of the hour. Sometimes we spend a lot of time talking about our kids, other times we plan family activities or share what we've been reading about lately. It's a pretty organic experience now, but when we first started, we definitely needed more structure.

Here's the agenda we started with:

1. Begin with a prayer. (If your spouse is open to praying together, definitely do that, but if not, say a prayer on your own before you get together. Better yet, do both. Then go through the questions below.)

2. What were your favorite things you (or we) did this week?

3. What did you most appreciate that others did for you?

4. What has gone well in our marriage, family, or work this week? CELEBRATE!

5. What's going on for you this week? Is there anything we need to put on the calendar?

6. What one thing would you like to do by yourself this week and how can I support you in doing it?

7. Do you have any ideas for family night or date night?
8. What would you like to eat this week?
9. Is there anything you learned recently that you would like to share?
10. Is there anything you would like me to work on that would make your life more pleasant? (By the way, don't ask this if you don't mean it, and don't get defensive if you don't like the answer! You don't have to do it. It's good information, though.)
11. Is there anything else you want to talk about? (This is the time for potentially touchy subjects.)

As with all other suggestions in this book, try experimenting with different ways to do your weekly meeting. See what works well for you. If having an agenda feels inauthentic and stilted, try some different ways to approach it so it feels more comfortable and repeatable. The weekly planning and talk time can be useful even if you are severely disconnected. Perhaps all you can manage is a five-minute conversation beginning with, "What's going on for you this week?" That's fine. You can build from there.

To get started, you can tell your spouse you'd like to have a planning date on Sundays (or whatever day you want to try). You may want to share the example of how my husband and I use the tradition, and how it continues to help us stay connected, work together, and consistently address any issues we're dealing with. If your spouse agrees, ask if he or she has any suggestions for making this an enjoyable tradition in your marriage.

When I first talked to my husband about having a weekly planning and talk time, he thought it would be a good thing for us to try. I showed him the formal agenda I had come up with and he agreed to go through the whole thing with me each week. We decided to get together on Sunday afternoons and start our discussion on positive topics. Then, we'd go through the rest of the list, ending with any touchy topics that we hadn't resolved during the week.

This arrangement worked well for about a year. At that point, I asked my husband if he had any suggestions for improving our "Sunday chats," as we had come to call them. He said that getting together around 3:00 was working fine for him, but he wanted to try taking a walk while we talked rather than sitting in his studio. He also told me that he didn't like the big binder I kept my notes in or the printed agenda we had been using.

Because of his input, I stopped using my binder and started using sticky notes. That way I could remember what I needed to bring up and I could still make a few notes of things we talked about. This change in approach worked beautifully until the weather got too cold. Then we went back to a sit-down chat, although we found it worked best when we talked at lunchtime rather than later in the afternoon.

As you can see, we've adjusted our approach several times, but we've continued to receive great benefits as we've kept the essence of this tradition. So just give it your best shot, and then adjust your approach until you discover a plan that works well for you. Keep adjusting as your needs change.

Recommended Resources and Helpful Quotations

Reading a few minutes a day is a great way to get new ideas and stay on track. Here are a few books, quotations, and online resources that have been helpful to me. I hope you find them to be interesting and supportive as well.

Books

1. Michele Weiner-Davis, *The Divorce Remedy: The Proven 7-Step Program for Saving Your Marriage* (New York, NY: Simon & Schuster, 2001).

   If you're only willing to read one book on marriage, this is my top pick. It's practical, action-oriented, positive, and fun to read. Michele does a great job of sharing stories as well as giving solid counselor-type advice.

   > People don't just fall out of love. If love dwindles, it's because the marriage wasn't a priority. Love is a living thing. If you nurture it, it grows. If you neglect it, it dies. ... Happily married people understand that if they engage in activities that bring love into the marriage, they will feel loving. (54)

   > Five Stages of Marriage: (1) Passion prevails. (2) What was I thinking?—"You knew life wouldn't always be a bed of roses, but you never thought all you'd get was a bed of thorns." (3) Everything would be great if *you* changed.—"In this stage of

marriage, most people believe that there are two ways of looking at things, your spouse's way, and your way, also known as the Right Way." (4) That's just the way my partner is.—"We dare to ask whether there's something about *our own behavior* that could use shaping up.... We stop being opponents. We're teammates again." (5) Together, at last.—"Since you are no longer in a struggle to define who you are and what the marriage should be, there is more peace and harmony." (59–64)

If you know how to push your partner's buttons in a negative way..., you can learn to push your partner's buttons in a positive way. (66)

Do nothing. Some people are fix-it addicts. Fixing their marriages becomes the main focus of their lives.... Sometimes the very best thing a fix-it addict can do is to back off and do nothing. (119–120)

Get a life.... When you feel desperate, you get clingy and depressed. You cry a lot, mope around, lose interest in things, and basically become a blob.... This isn't the *real you*.... Ask yourself, "What was it about me that attracted my spouse to me in the first place?... You're acting differently right now because you're going through hell, not because you've changed radically as a person.... Remember *who you really are*.... Become more upbeat in your partner's presence. (127–128)

2. John M. Gottman and Nan Silver, *The Seven Principles for Making Marriage Work: A Practical Guide from the Country's Foremost Relationship Expert* (New York, NY: Harmony Books, 1999, 2015).

This is a close second pick. It isn't as positive since it includes several stories about people who end up getting divorced. However, it has a lot of great information. It was very helpful for me and I recommend it to anyone wanting to improve his or her marriage.

Turn Toward Each Other Instead of Away. . . . Couples are always making what I call 'bids' for each other's attention, affection, humor, or support. Bids can be as minor as asking for a back rub or as significant as seeking help in carrying the burden when an aging parent is ill. The partner responds to each bid either by *turning toward* the spouse or *turning away*. A tendency to turn toward your partner is the basis of trust, emotional connection, passion, and a satisfying sex life. . . . Couples who remained married had turned toward their partner's bids an average of 86 percent of the time in the Love Lab, while those who ended up divorced had averaged only 33 percent. . . . Each time partners turn toward each other, they are funding . . . their *emotional bank account*. They are building up savings that, like money in the bank, can serve as a cushion when times get rough. . . . Because they have stored an abundance of goodwill, such couples are less likely to teeter over into distrust and chronic negativity during hard times. (88–89, italics added)

There is no such thing as constructive criticism. All criticism is painful. Unlike complaints—specific requests for change—criticism doesn't make a marriage better. It inevitably makes it worse. (282)

[This is] what goes wrong 85 percent of the time in marriages. If you consider yourself inadequate, you are always on the lookout for what is not there in yourself and your partner. . . . The problem is that we tend to focus on what's missing in our mate and overlook the fine qualities that are there—we take those for granted. . . . Expressions of thanksgiving and praise are the antidotes to the poison of criticism and its deadly cousin, contempt. (283)

The more you can imbue your relationship with the spirit of thanksgiving and the graceful presence of praise, the more profound and fulfilling your lives together will be. (284)

3. Fawn Weaver, *Happy Wives Club: One Woman's Worldwide Search for the Secrets of a Great Marriage* (Nashville, TN: Nelson Books, 2014).

Happy Wives Club is a travel log. It's a cozy-up-to-the-fire-with-a-cup-of-tea kind of book. Fawn travels the world in search of happy marriages and what they have in common. Most of the book is about her journey to different continents, her thoughts as she travels, the couples she meets, and their stories. At the very end of the book, she shares what the happily-married couples have in common.

> "When you have a problem, you have to fight together," Estrellita told us . . . "That is the problem: most of the time couples don't want to fight together. They fight against each other." (211)

> Twelve Secrets of a Great Marriage: Respect, Trust, Belief in God, Laughter is the best medicine, Keep outside interests, Create a daily ritual, Date your spouse, Support your spouse, Friendship is Essential, Nurture your marriage, No Plan B, Choose your friends wisely. (See pages 247–249.)

> Keep outside interests. . . . Each couple (especially the wives) pointed out the importance of having interests (hobbies, work, etc.) outside of the home and outside of their family. A separate identity is important and keeps each person from 'smothering' the other or becoming bored with the other. (247)

> No Plan B . . . Divorce is not an option so we will figure things out, even if it takes time. We've got time! (247)

> Choose your friends wisely. . . . Surrounding yourself with others who build up your marriage rather than attempt to tear it down was a must. (249)

4. Fawn Weaver, *The Argument-Free Marriage: 28 Days to Creating the Marriage You've Always Wanted with the Spouse You Already Have* (Nashville, TN: Nelson Books, 2015).

The Argument-Free Marriage presents principles, ideas, and suggestions for marriage improvement. I found the book interesting, fun to read, and full of good ideas. Fawn goes through 28 suggestions, intending for the reader to read and apply one chapter each day. Many of her suggestions are concepts from the Happy Wives Club but with the approach being to help readers apply, not just discover, the concepts. Among other things, she talks about why couples argue and how to stop arguing, about dreaming new dreams, about checking out your lifestyle, and about figuring out finances.

> Every couple I've interviewed (happily married twenty-five-plus years)—from North America to South America, Africa to Europe, Asia to Australia—has a daily ritual. They make the time to do something together each and every day. Nothing fancy. Not necessarily getting dressed up or spending money at a restaurant. Nor spending hours in the kitchen trying to cook the perfect meal or dusting off the china. What these couples did was simple. (92)

> One of the greatest benefits of keeping a gratitude list is that it serves as a constant reminder of what makes your spouse so awesome. It's a constant reminder of why, out of all the people in the world, you chose your spouse. During those times when your imperfections glare brighter than your attributes . . . look at your gratitude list to be reminded that your marriage is bigger than that moment of discouragement. (109)

> The real fun comes in when you begin looking for things to add to your [gratitude] list. You will be amazed at how many considerate and helpful things your spouse does that you may have otherwise overlooked. And if your spouse is anything like mine, you'll soon realize there aren't enough thank-yous in a day. (111)

5. John M. Gottman and Joan DeClaire, *The Relationship Cure: A 5 Step Guide to Strengthening Your Marriage, Family, and Friendships* (New York, NY: Harmony Books, 2001).

This is another good book by John Gottman. It is a practical program with ideas and exercises to transform troubled relationships into positive ones. It includes suggestions for sixteen marriage rituals.

> Rituals are repeated, predictable events that have symbolic meaning. A ritual can be really simple, like a peck on the cheek as you rush off to work, or quite elaborate, like a wedding. When rituals of emotional connection are done well in a marriage, they help married couples celebrate their bond and stay together through all kinds of trials and triumphs. . . .
>
> **Leave-taking.** Before you part company, find out at least one thing that's going to happen in your partner's life that day. That will give you something to talk about when you get home.
>
> **Affectionate greetings and partings.** Share a loving kiss when departing or coming back together again. . . .
>
> **Mealtimes.** Sit down at the table to share your meals. Turn off the television. . . . Talk about the events of the day in ways that are supportive, affectionate, and encouraging. . . .
>
> **Dates.** Get out and do something enjoyable as a couple, without kids or other adults around. Make sure that at least part of the date includes time for talking. (240–242)
>
> A married couple's life can get so busy with work and family responsibilities that unless they plan a time to make love and have a ritual surrounding it, the lovemaking never happens. Or it only happens late at night when both partners are exhausted and it's not so much fun. So I recommend that couples ritualize lovemaking to make sure it happens regularly and in a way that both partners find exciting. . . . Think about the effort you made early in your relationship to make sex as pleasurable as possible. Perhaps certain music, perfume, lingerie, or candlelight helped you to set the

mood. If you've let such preparations fall by the wayside, bring them back to your relationship. ... Pay attention to the rituals your partner finds most exciting, and use those often. (242–243)

6. John M. Gottman, *Why Marriages Succeed or Fail: And how you can make yours last* (New York, NY: Simon & Schuster, 1994).

This is one of John Gottman's first books. It focuses on attitudes that doom marriages and ways to avoid patterns that lead to divorce.

> The Magic Ratio. ... We carefully charted the amount of time couples spent fighting versus interacting positively—touching, smiling, paying compliments, laughing, etc. ... [The] magic ratio is 5 to 1. ... As long as there is five times as much positive feeling and interaction between husband and wife as there is negative, we found the marriage was likely to be stable. ... Your marriage needs much more positivity than negativity to nourish your love. Without it, your relationship is in danger of withering and dying. ... Couples who were headed for a breakup ... showed slightly more negative than positive acts. (56–57)

> The first cascade a couple hits as they tumble down the marital rapids is comprised of 'The Four Horsemen of the Apocalypse,' my name for four disastrous ways of interacting that sabotage your attempts to communicate with your partner. In order of least to most dangerous, they are *criticism, contempt, defensiveness,* and *stonewalling*. As these behaviors become more and more entrenched, husband and wife focus increasingly on the escalating sense of negativity and tension in their marriage. Eventually they may become deaf to each other's efforts at peacemaking. (72)

7. Stephen R. Covey, *The 7 Habits of Highly Effective People: Powerful Lessons in Personal Change* (New York, NY: Simon & Schuster, 1989, 2004).

The 7 Habits is a classic. It's one of the best books I've ever read on personal transformation and effectiveness. If you haven't read it, yet, I invite you to do so. If you have read it, but it's been a while, you might want to review the seven habits again.

> If you want to *have* a happy marriage, *be* the kind of person who generates positive energy and sidesteps negative energy rather than empowering it. (51)

> At one seminar where I was speaking . . . , a man came up and said, "My wife and I just don't have the same feelings for each other we used to have. I guess I just don't love her anymore and she doesn't love me. What can I do?" . . .
> "Love her. . . . Love is a verb. Love—the feeling—is a fruit of love, the verb. So love her. Serve her. Sacrifice. Listen to her. Empathize. Appreciate. Affirm her. Are you willing to do that?" (87)

> An Emotional Bank Account is a metaphor that describes the amount of trust that's been built up in a relationship. . . . If I make deposits . . . with you through courtesy, kindness, honesty, and keeping my commitments to you, I build up a reserve. . . . But if I have a habit of showing discourtesy, disrespect, cutting you off, overreacting, ignoring you, becoming arbitrary, betraying your trust, or playing little tin god in your life, eventually my Emotional Bank Account is overdrawn. The trust level gets very low. . . . If a large reserve of trust is not sustained by continuing deposits, a marriage will deteriorate. (198)

> Go out with your spouse on a regular basis. Have dinner or do something together you both enjoy. Listen to each other; seek to understand. See life through each other's eyes. (270)

8. Marshall Rosenberg, *Living Nonviolent Communication: Practical Tools to Connect and Communicate Skillfully in Every Situation* (Sounds True, Inc., Boulder, CO, 2012).

The basics of NVC are to honestly self-connect, recognize your true feelings, figure out what needs those feelings point to, and come up with healthy ways to meet those needs. It's all about personal responsibility and how to connect at a deep level with yourself and others around you so that you experience more depth and vibrance in your life. While I haven't found NVC to be the "end all, be all" for me, I like the mindset and use the skills on a regular basis to help me self-connect and connect well with others. You can find several short videos of Marshall on YouTube as well as a full nine-hour training listed below in the Online Resources section.

> Nonviolent Communication, or NVC, is a powerful model of communication, but it goes far beyond that. It is a way of being, thinking, and living in the world. Its purpose is to inspire heartfelt connections between ourselves and other people—connections that allow everyone's needs to be met through compassionate giving. It inspires us and others to give from the heart. It also helps us connect to our inner divinity and to what is alive in us moment to moment. (vii)

> When it comes to managing anger, NVC shows how to use anger as an alarm that tells us we are thinking in ways that are not likely to get our needs met. . . . What we want to do as we use NVC to manage anger is to go more deeply into it, to see what is going on within us when we are angry, to be able to get at the need—which is the root of anger—and then fulfill that need. . . . [It's] similar to the warning light on the dashboard of a car—it's providing useful information about what the engine needs. Your wouldn't want to hide or disconnect or ignore it. You'd want to slow down the car and figure out what the light's trying to tell you. (95–96)

> I think it is important that people see that spirituality is at the base of Nonviolent Communication and that they learn the mechanics of the NVC process with that in mind. It's really a spiritual practice that I am trying to show as a way of life. (143)

> Nonviolent Communication really came out of my attempt to understand this concept of love and how to manifest it, how to do it. (146)

9. Michele Weiner-Davis, *Divorce Busting: A Step-by-Step Approach to Making Your Marriage Loving Again* (New York, NY: Fireside, 1992)

Michele's first book, Divorce Busting, has helped many couples restore their love and save their marriages. She illustrates her marriage-enriching techniques with helpful examples of couples she has worked with in her marriage and family therapy practice. The examples make it easy to understand and apply the techniques.

> If cheering up a depressed person makes her more depressed, if asking for more closeness from an aloof person makes him more withdrawn, if pleading for more reassurance about commitment leads to a breach of commitment, why do we persist in doing what doesn't work. Why don't we quit doing the same old thing and try something else, anything else? (103)

> If it doesn't work, do something different. . . . It is essential that you approach solution finding with a researcher's mind: Experiment with something new and carefully note your mate's response. If it appears that the new approach is helping you reach your goal, keep it up. If not, try a different approach. Marriage enhancement . . . is a trial-and-error process. Don't be discouraged if one method doesn't work—try another one. I once heard it said, "There is no such thing as failure, just useful feedback about what to do next." (141–142)

> Do a 180°. ... If ... you have noticed that your efforts to fix things have only made things worse, you might try to do a 180°. ... This technique is a variation of technique number one—do anything different. It differs in that instead of trying anything new it directs you to specifically do the opposite of what you've been doing. (160–163)

Online Resources

1. HappyWivesClub.com

   This is Fawn Weaver's website. I love it! It's full of good quotes, articles, and ideas for how to create a joyful marriage and celebrate it regularly. Connecting with the Happy Wives Club website and Fawn's social media sites is a good way to surround yourself with uplifting and happily married people.

   Fawn currently has twelve categories for visitors to look into. (1) Daily Marriage—Creating the marriage of your dreams day-by-day. (2) Positive Marriage Graphics—Best love and happy marriage memes on the web. (3) Date Ideas—Fun, Free and Frugal Date Ideas for Day or Night. (4) "Just Because" & Anniversary Gift Ideas for Your Spouse. (5) Happy Webstore where you can get Fawn's books and a few other items. (6) Better Sex & Flirting—Spice up your marriage with these sexy tips. (7) Traveling with Your Spouse. (8) Health & Fitness. (9) Yummy Recipes. (10) 12 Weeks to Happier Marriage. (11) 21 Days to a Happier You. (12) Most Popular Articles.

   Here are a few of my favorite quotes on Happy Wives Club.

   > A successful marriage requires falling in love many times, always with the same person. —Mignon McLaughlin

> A happy marriage is the union of two good forgivers.
> —Robert Quillen
>
> A great marriage is not when the 'perfect couple' comes together. It is when an imperfect couple learns to enjoy their differences. —Dave Meurer
>
> Marriage doesn't make you happy—you make your marriage happy. —Drs. Les and Leslie Parrott
>
> One of the greatest gifts you can give your husband is your own wholeness. —Stormie Omartian
>
> Happily ever after is not a fairy tale. It's a choice. —Fawn Weaver
>
> Don't ever confuse a great marriage with a perfect one. A great marriage is attained through daily effort, love and investment of time. A perfect marriage doesn't exist because it involves the union of two imperfect people. —Fawn Weaver

2. MorningLightCounseling.com

   This is Carrie Wrigley's professional website.

   > Morning Light Counseling is a resource designed to extend light and hope in the midst of stormy, perilous times. While much is amiss in the world, there is much to celebrate, much to rejoice in. *"Weeping may endure for a night, but joy cometh in the morning."* (Psalms 30:5)

3. CounselingLibrary.com

   > Carrie [Wrigley] . . . operates this online resource library featuring articles, books, handouts, and other resources on a wide range of topics. This sister site [to MorningLightCounseling.com] contains much more information about the kinds of approaches Carrie takes in therapy, and provides resources for Carrie's clients to help

themselves between sessions, and to continue to help themselves stay well and happy, once therapy is concluded.

The Library is also open to the public, as a public service, to assist people around the world in locating information to help themselves and their loved ones resolve personal, relationship, and family challenges. The Library also contains information on building wellness and resilience, to make the emergence or re-emergence of these problems less likely. (This description is found on MorningLightCounseling.com's homepage)

Here is an excerpt from an article titled "Giving Focus and Attention to Your Spouse" by Carrie M. Wrigley:

"What does not get cared for consistently becomes a problem over time." We see this with gardens, cars, dishes, and children. If we neglect to provide continuous needed care to something or someone, over time, almost always, it becomes a problem. Our relationships are no different. Unwatered plants die, and cars we forget to fuel and change the oil on begin to sputter and fail over time.

So often, the longer we are together, the more we may be inclined to take each other for granted, and give other things primary focus. This might be the job, the kids, the religion, the hobby, or the "must-see TV" or ongoing torrent of social media chatter. If we do not make special, dedicated effort to care diligently for our marriages, they can become spindly and frail, and ultimately fail. . . .

[However,] You don't have to flood a potted flower to keep it alive and vibrant. You don't have to change the oil in your car every day to keep it running smoothly. And you don't have to give your spouse 100% of your time and attention every day. But give 100% of your focus and attention for at least part of every day. Share your love, extend yourself in kindness to your partner. Before long, you will realize that "Stage Three" [mature love] can be every bit as joyful as "Stage One" [the honeymoon phase]—if not more so, because of the richness and synergy of all the diverse pieces—the grand kaleidoscope your lives entail at that point.

We enjoy, in our time, more opportunities and more options than any previous generation of human beings. This can bring great danger to our close relationships—or, it can bring vastly expanded growth and enjoyment. Protect your marriage—cultivate and nourish it intentionally—and it can remain strong, joyful, and unified. (https://goo.gl/8ij77Y or http://counselinglibrary.org/relationships/strengthening-marriage/giving-focus-attention-to-spouse)

4. Nonviolent Communication (NVC) Resources

"Nonviolent Communication Training Course Marshall Rosenberg CNVC org" is a nine hour audio training course posted on YouTube where Marshall dives deeply into each aspect of NVC. The nine parts are: An Introduction, Applying NVC, Honesty, Empathy Part One, Relationships, Authority, Empathy Part Two, Social Change, and Sincere Gratitude Requests.

> Nonviolent communication consists of a value system that we are trying to live by and then it outlines a language, thinking, communication skills, and means of influence that support that way of living. (Go to https://goo.gl/4LaFZ9 or https://www.youtube.com/watch?v=O4tUVqsjQ2I.)

Notes

1. John M. Gottman and Nan Silver, *The Seven Principles for Making Marriage Work: A Practical Guide from the Country's Foremost Relationship Expert* (New York, NY: Harmony Books, 1999, 2015), 22–23.

2. Stephen R. Covey, *The 7 Habits of Highly Effective People: Powerful Lessons in Personal Change* (New York, NY: Simon & Schuster, 1989, 2004), 198–212.

3. Gottman and Silver, 127.

4. Gottman and Silver, 280.

5. Michele Weiner-Davis, *The Divorce Remedy: The Proven 7-Step Program for Saving Your Marriage* (New York, NY: Simon & Schuster, 2001), 69, italics added.

6. Marshal B. Rosenberg, *Nonviolent Communication: A Language of Life* (Encinitas, CA: PuddleDancer Press, 2016).

7. John M. Gottman, *Why Marriages Succeed or Fail: And How You Can Make Yours Last* (New York, NY: Simon & Schuster, 1994), 56–57.

8. Gottman and Silver, 87–114.

9. John M. Gottman and Joan DeClaire, *The Relationship Cure: A 5 Step Guide to Strengthening Your Marriage, Family, and Friendships* (New York, NY: Harmony Books, 1999, 2015), 242–243.

10. Gottman and Silver, 279.

11. Kerry Patterson, Joseph Grenny, David Maxfield, Ron McMillan, and Al Switzler, *Change Anything: The New Science of Personal Success* (New York, NY: Business Plus, 2011), 43.

12. http://counselinglibrary.org/relationships/strengthening-marriage/giving-focus-attention-to-spouse

13. Gottman and Silver, 179–184.

14. Weiner-Davis, 127–129. John M. Gottman, Julie Schwartz Gottman, and Joan DeClaire, *Ten Lessons to Transform Your Marriage: America's Love Lab Experts Share Their Strategies for Strengthening Your Relationship* (New York, NY: Crown Publishing Group), 86–88.

15. Gottman, *Why Marriages Succeed or Fail:*, 56–57.

Index

Attitude, 41

Books
  Argument-Free Marriage, 90
  Divorce Busting, 94
  Divorce Remedy, 85
  E^2: Nine Do-It-Yourself Energy Experiments, 47
  Happy Wives Club:, 88
  Living Nonviolent Communication, 93
  Relationship Cure, 91
  7 Habits of Highly Effective People, 92
  Seven Principles for Making Marriage Work, 86
  Why Marriages Succeed or Fail:, 91

Carrie Wrigley, 20, 25, 26, 32, 65, 77, 106
Compassionate Communication, 19, 27, 93, 94, 98

Daily Connection Plan, 73, 77, 78
  Adjusting, 79
  Designing, 59
  Example, 60

Emotional Bank Account, 12, 26, 30, 77, 81, 87, 92

Fawn Weaver, 88, 89
Five Stages of Marriage, 85
Flooding, 69

Gratitude, 37, 49, 54, 57, 87, 89

Happily Ever After, 11, 12, 71
HappyWivesClub.com, 95
Husband, defined, 13

John Gottman, 11, 15, 25, 86, 90, 91
  Flooding, 69
  Magic Ratio, 77

Love Log, 35, 37, 76
  Be a Scientist, 61
  Customizing Your Love Log, 67
  Format, 53
  Reviewing and Adjusting Your Plan, 62
  Sample Pages, 56
  What to Record, 53

Magic Ratio, 25, 91
Marshall Rosenberg, 19, 26, 93, 98

Michele Weiner-Davis, 16, 85, 94
   Five Stages of Marriage, 85
Mindset Mantras, 42, 76
My Story, 5

Nonviolent Communication, 19, 26, 94, 98
   Basic Ideas, 93

Orange Butterflies
   Looking for good things in your marriage, 47–49

Personalizing Your Love Log, 45

Quotations
   Love is a living thing. If you nurture it, it grows. If you neglect it, it dies., 85
   Love may be blind, but marriage is a real eye opener!, 3
   Marriage is the hardest work you'll ever do, but it is also the best work you'll ever do., 3
   More than 80 percent of the time, it's the wife who brings up sticky marital issues., 15
   People don't just fall out of love. If love dwindles, it's because the marriage wasn't a priority., 85
   The greater the struggle, the more glorious the triumph!, 31
   There is no such thing as constructive criticism. All criticism is painful., 87
   There is no such thing as failure, just useful feedback about what to do next., 94
   We don't have to be perfect to be perfect for each other., 3
   When you tip over the first domino in your marriage, relationship change will be right around the corner., 16
   You can't put your marriage on cruise control., 64
   You don't have to flood a potted flower to keep it alive and vibrant., 65, 97

Rituals, 90

Save-cation, 66
Self-Care, 44
Sexual Intimacy, 31, 80
   Scheduling regularly, 34
Stephen Covey, 12, 92
Surround Yourself with Happily Married Couples, 73, 88

The 4 T's, 20–34, 71, 80
   Talk, 24–27, 80, 81
   Time, 21–24, 80, 81
   Touch, 31–34, 80
   Trust, 27–30, 80
Touch and Gender Differences, 31
Triggers, 69
Turning Toward Each Other, 28–30, 73, 87
Twelve Secrets of a Great Marriage, 88

Weekly Planning and Talk Time, 60, 81
Wife, defined, 13

Acknowledgments

Thanks goes to my husband for having the commitment and character to stick with me on the long and bumpy road to our *happily ever after*. I sure love you, Babe.

Thanks to my parents for their constant support and belief in me and in my work. Without you, I would never have made it this far. Thank you so much for everything!

Thanks to Carrie Wrigley for all of her help and encouragement with this book.

Thanks to Jennie Williams for the cover and interior design and to Katie Stirling of Eschler Editing for the editing.

Thanks to all my friends and coaches at Quantum Leap, especially Martha Bullen and Geoffrey Berwind. I love you guys.

www.ingramcontent.com/pod-product-compliance
Lightning Source LLC
Chambersburg PA
CBHW031407040426
42444CB00005B/451